THE CIVIL WAR

A VISUAL HISTORY

Rare Images and Tales of the War Between the States

PaRragon

Bath · New York · Cologne · Melbourne · Delhi
Hong Kong · Shenzhen · Singapore · Amsterdam

This edition published by Parragon Books Ltd in 2015 and distributed by

Parragon Inc.
440 Park Avenue South, 13th Floor
New York, NY 10016
www.parragon.com

Copyright © Parragon Books Ltd 2011-2015

ISBN: 978-1-4454-9922-2

Printed in China

CONTENTS

THE CONFLICT BEGINS

May God protect our country in these perilous times. There is a strong Secession element in this city and the lines may be drawn pretty close with us but I will in all emergencies stand by the old Stars & Stripes while the vital current flows through my veins.

– Watson B. Smith, 8th Cavalry, Michigan

A geographical line has been drawn across the Union, and all the States north of that line have united in the election of a man to the high office of President of the United States, whose opinions and purposes are hostile to slavery. He is to be entrusted with the administration of the common Government, because he has declared that that "Government cannot endure permanently half slave, half free," and that the public mind must rest in the belief that slavery is in the course of ultimate extinction.

– South Carolina Convention, December 24, 1860

Photograph shows participants and crowd at the first inauguration of President Abraham Lincoln, at the U.S. Capitol, Washington, D.C. Lincoln is standing under the wood canopy, at the front, midway between the left and center posts. His face is in shadow but the white shirtfront is visible. March 4, 1861.

THE CONFLICT BEGINS

I have not allowed myself, Sir, to look beyond the Union, to see what might lie hidden in the dark recess behind. I have not cooly weighed the chances of preserving liberty when the bonds that unite us together shall be broken asunder. I have not accustomed myself to hang over the precipice of disunion, to see whether, with my short sight, I can fathom the depth of the abyss below; nor could I regard him as a safe counselor in the affairs of this government, whose thoughts should be mainly bent on considering, not how the Union may be best preserved, but how tolerable might be the condition of the people when it should be broken up and destroyed.

Daniel Webster, January 26, 1830

$100 REWARD!
RANAWAY

From the undersigned, living on Current River, about twelve miles above Doniphan, in Ripley County, Mo., on 2nd of March, 1860, **A NE GRO MAN,** about 30 years old, weighs about 160 pounds; high forehead, with a scar on it; had on brown pants and coat very much worn, and an old black wool hat; shoes size No. 11.

The above reward will be given to any person who may apprehend this said negro out of the State; and fifty dollars if apprehended in this State outside of Ripley county, or $25 if taken in Ripley county.

APOS TUCKER.

INSPECTION AND SALE OF A NEGRO.

Lincoln campaign button

South Carolina is anxiously desirous of living at peace with her brethren; she has not the remotest wish to dissolve the political bands which have connected her with the great American family of confederated States. With Thomas Jefferson, "she would regard the dissolution of our Union with them as one of the greatest of evils—but not the greatest: there is one greater—submission to a Government without limitation of powers"; and such a Government, she conscientiously believes, will be our portion, should the system against which she is now struggling be finally established as the settled policy of the country.

South Carolina is solicitous to preserve the Constitution as our fathers framed it—according to its true spirit, intent, and meaning; but she is inflexibly determined never to surrender her reserved rights, nor to suffer the constitutional compact to be converted into an instrument for the oppression of her citizens.

Governor Robert Hayne, South Carolina inaugural speech, December 13, 1830

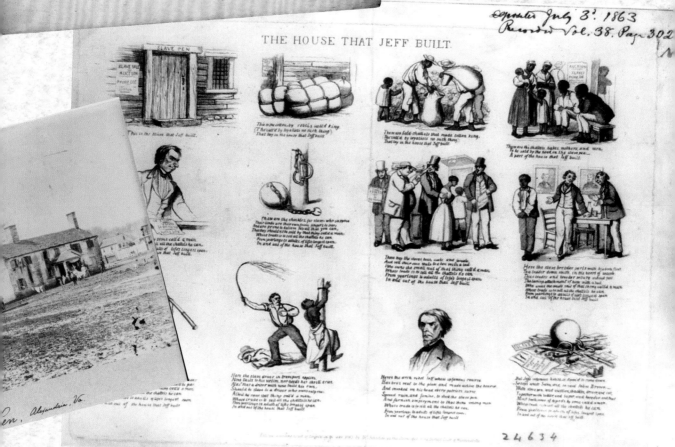

THE HOUSE THAT JEFF BUILT.

Years ago I was convinced that the Southern States would be compelled either to separate from the North, by dissolving the Federal Government, or they would be compelled to abolish the institution of African Slavery. This, in my judgment, was the only alternative; and I foresaw that the South would be compelled, at some day, to make her selection. The day is now come, and Alabama must make her selection, either to secede from the Union, and assume the position of a sovereign, independent State, or she must submit to a system of policy on the part of the Federal Government that, in a short time, will compel her to abolish African Slavery.

This being the alternative, I cannot hesitate for a moment what my duty is. I must separate from the Government of my fathers, the one under which I have lived, and under which I wished to die. But I must do my duty to my country and my fellow beings; and humanity, in my judgment, demands that Alabama should separate herself from the Government of the United States.

Speech of E.S. Dargan
Secession Convention of Alabama,
January 11, 1861

Secession Hall

The inauguration of Jefferson Davis

Jefferson Davis, President of the Confederate States of America

THE STARTING POINT OF THE GREAT WAR BETWEEN THE STATES.
INAUGURATION OF JEFFERSON DAVIS

The first flag of independence raised in the South by the citizens of Savannah, Georgia

2, Langham Chambers.
All Souls Place.
Portland Place.
London. W.

This is to certify that the Great Seal of the Confederate States of America was engraved by my uncle, Mr Joseph S. Wyon, and that an original impression of this seal is in my studio, it being the practice of our house to preserve proof impressions of all Seals executed by us during the past 70 years.

I further certify that the reproduction of the Great Seal of the Confederate States, 1861-1865, made and copyrighted by Annie Payne Pillow in 1911, has been carefully compared by me with the above mentioned proof impression of the Great Seal in my studio, and that I find the reproduction to be a careful and accurate reproduction of the Great Seal.

(signed) Allan G. Wyon

20th April. 1912.

Medallist and Engraver to His Majesty the King of England

Top: Letter that accompanied The Great Seal of the Confederacy to the Library of Congress

Bottom right: Confederate money

THE CONFLICT BEGINS

THE CONQUERED BANNER—WAVING FREE IN '61

The first Confederate flag made in Augusta, Georgia, swells in the May breeze of 1861. It has two red bars, with a white in the middle, and a union of blue with seven stars. The men who so proudly stand before it near the armory at Macon are the Clinch Rifles, forming Company A of the Fifth Georgia Infantry. The organization was completed on the next day—May 11th. It first went to Pensacola. From after the battle of Shiloh to July, 1864, it served in the Army of Tennessee, when it was sent to the Georgia coast, later serving under General Joseph E. Johnston in the final campaign in the Carolinas. It was conspicuous at Chickamauga, where its colonel commanded a brigade. His account of the action on September 20, 1863, is well worth quoting: "The brigade, with the battery in the center, moved forward in splendid style about 100 yards, when the enemy opened a galling fire from the front and left flank, enfilading the entire

[245]

"ONCE TEN THOUSANDS HAILED IT GLADLY"

line with canister and small-arms. The engagement now became terrific and the position of my brigade extremely critical. The troops, however, stood nobly to the work before them, and, steadily advancing, surmounted the hill on which the enemy's breastworks were, the battery moving with the line, and rendering effective service. The enemy were driven from their breastworks, and Brigadier-General Maney's brigade coming up at this opportune moment, charged them, and the contest was over. At daylight on Monday morning the enemy was found to have sought safety in flight under the cover of darkness." During the battle the regiment lost 194 men, a percentage of 54.95. The next highest recorded loss was 42.78. Ryan's words, "Those who once unrolled it," can appropriately be quoted under this spirited scene. And another phrase, "Cold and dead are lying now," fits too sadly well the careers of these volunteers from Georgia.

Top: The unveiling of the Confederate flag.
Right and bottom:The Great Seal of the Confederate States of America

Resolved by the Congress of the Confederate States of America,

That the Seal of the Confederate States shall consist of a device representing an equestrian portrait of Washington (after the statue which surmounts his monument in the Capitol Square at Richmond), surrounded with a wreath composed of the principal agricultural products of the Confederacy (cotton, tobacco, sugar-cane, corn, wheat and rice) and having around its margin the words: "The Confederate States of America, Twenty-second February, Eighteen Hundred and Sixty-two," with the following motto: "Deo Vindice."

Designed by the late Thomas J. Semmes, of Louisiana, Engraved by the late Joseph S. Wyon, Chief Engraver of Her Majesty's Seals, London, England

BATTLES

✝

FIGHTING TO DO

In aiming the first gun fired against the rebellion I had no feeling of self-reproach, for I fully believed that the contest was inevitable and was not of our seeking. The United States was called upon not only to defend its sovereignty, but its right to exist as a nation. The only alternative was to submit to a powerful oligarchy who were determined to make freedom forever subordinate to slavery. To me it was simply a contest, politically speaking, as to whether virtue or vice should rule.

–Reminiscences of Fort Sumter *by Abner Doubleday*

The Convention has adjourned. Now he tells me the attack on Fort Sumter may begin tonight; depends upon Anderson and the fleet outside. I do not pretend to go to sleep. How can I? If Anderson does not accept terms at four, the orders are, he shall be fired upon. I count to four, St. Michael's bells chime out and I begin to hope. At half-past four the heavy booming of a cannon. I sprang out of bed, and on my knees prostrate I prayed as I never prayed before.

–A Diary from Dixie *by Mary Boykin Miller Chestnut*

Confederates firing on Fort Sumter

FORT SUMTER
DECEMBER 9TH 1863
View of entrance to Three Gun Batys.

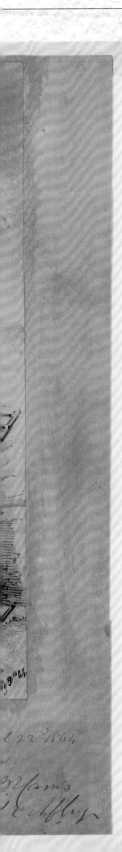

THE DEMAND FOR THE SURRENDER OF NEW ORLEANS.

Top: *The demand for the surrender of New Orleans*

Bottom: *Attack on the Massachusetts 6th, at Baltimore, April 19, 1861*

ATTACK ON THE MASSACHUSETTS 6th AT BALTIMORE
APRIL 19th 1861

Entered according to Act of Congress
in the Year 1885 by the
McCORMICK HARVESTING MACHINE Co.
in the Office of the
Librarian of Congress at Washington

·BATTLE OF SHILOH·APRIL

THE McCORMICK MACHINES COME VICTORIOUSLY OUT OF EVERY CONTEST, AND WITHOU

·PRESENTED WITH COMPLIMENTS OF·McCORMICK HARVESTING MACHINE COMPANY·

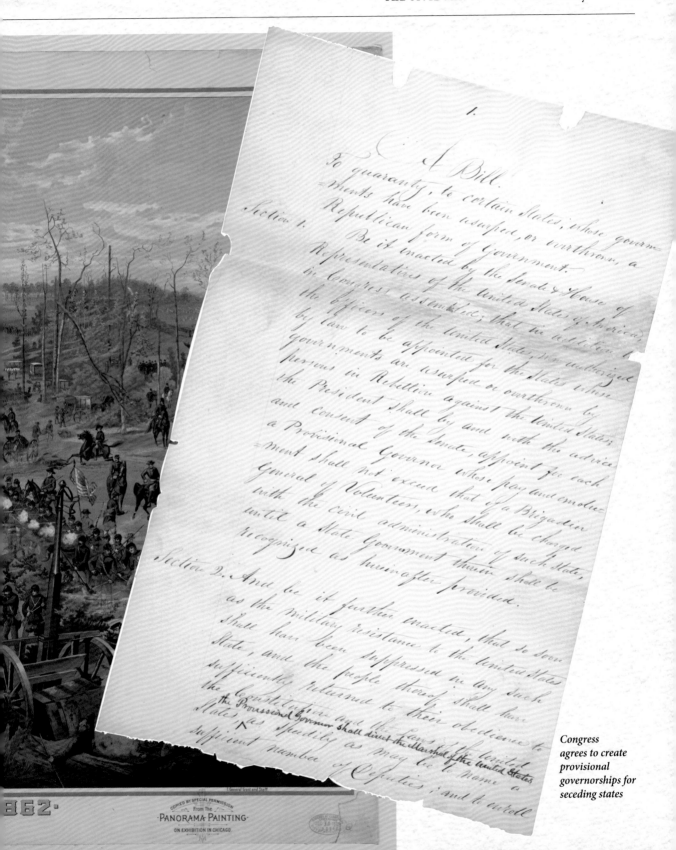

Congress agrees to create provisional governorships for seceding states

CENTREVILLE, VA., Dec. 22, 1861

There was a battle fought a few miles above here day before yesterday, in which our side was considerably worsted. One of the regiments of my brigade was in it, the Sixth regiment. They lost eighty-three men killed and wounded. Some of the regiment fared even worse than that. They are now bringing some of the dead here to bury them. I hear them playing the dead march at the cemetery. Oh, how lonesome!

I have been again to-day to visit the old battlefield. I never want to see it again. I saw the stump I got behind for a while that day, thinking it might shelter me a little, but if a cannon ball had hit it, it would have torn the stump and me, too, all to pieces, and some of them did not miss it very far. The stump is about ten inches high and nearly rotton. A drowning man will catch at a straw. My whole company was lying down at the time I am speaking of. It was while we were on the hill in front of Stone Bridge.

As many as eight at a time can get furlough now to go home, but I positively don't want one when I come home. I want to remain a while. Christmas will soon be here and then the 14th of April will quickly follow. I send some money in this letter. Do with it as you think best.

Yours as ever, J. W. REID

Sudley church through the trees, Bull Run, Virginia

Interior of Fort Sumter during the bombardment, April 12th, 1861

Breaching battery against Fort Sumter

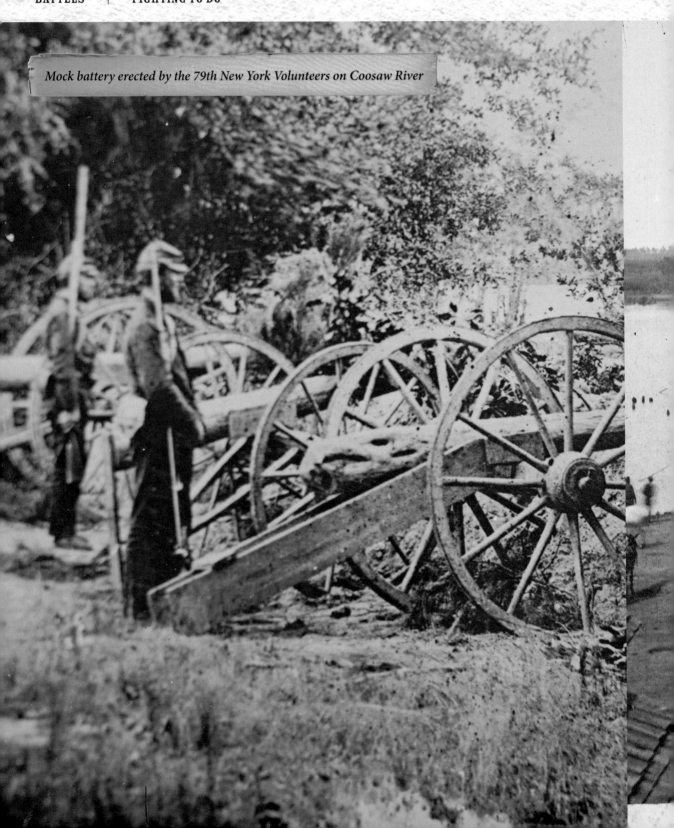

Mock battery erected by the 79th New York Volunteers on Coosaw River

Port Royal evacuation

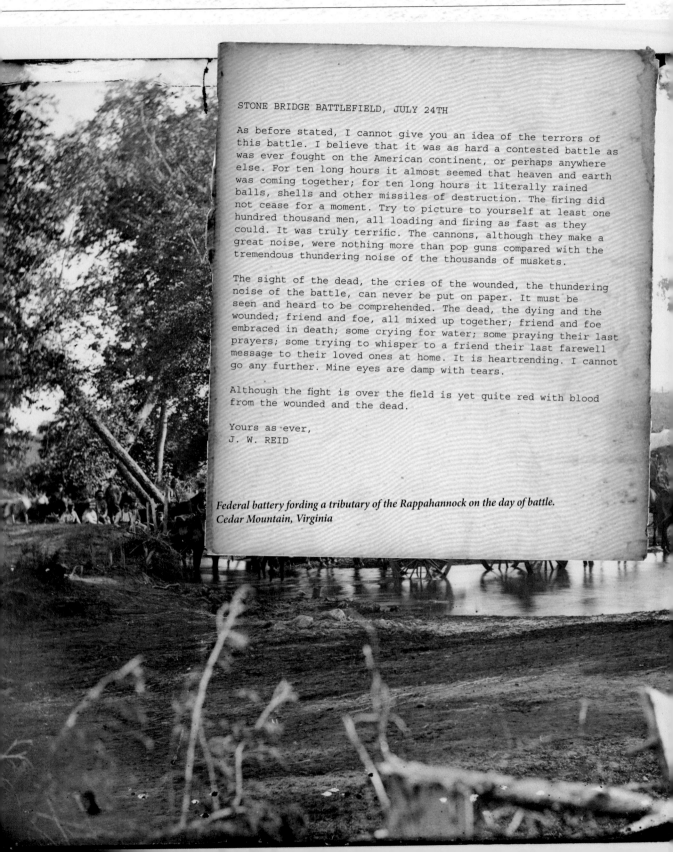

STONE BRIDGE BATTLEFIELD, JULY 24TH

As before stated, I cannot give you an idea of the terrors of this battle. I believe that it was as hard a contested battle as was ever fought on the American continent, or perhaps anywhere else. For ten long hours it almost seemed that heaven and earth was coming together; for ten long hours it literally rained balls, shells and other missiles of destruction. The firing did not cease for a moment. Try to picture to yourself at least one hundred thousand men, all loading and firing as fast as they could. It was truly terrific. The cannons, although they make a great noise, were nothing more than pop guns compared with the tremendous thundering noise of the thousands of muskets.

The sight of the dead, the cries of the wounded, the thundering noise of the battle, can never be put on paper. It must be seen and heard to be comprehended. The dead, the dying and the wounded; friend and foe, all mixed up together; friend and foe embraced in death; some crying for water; some praying their last prayers; some trying to whisper to a friend their last farewell message to their loved ones at home. It is heartrending. I cannot go any further. Mine eyes are damp with tears.

Although the fight is over the field is yet quite red with blood from the wounded and the dead.

Yours as ever,
J. W. REID

Federal battery fording a tributary of the Rappahannock on the day of battle.
Cedar Mountain, Virginia

FRONT LINES

★ ★ ★ ★ ★ ★ ★ ★ ★ ★ ★ ★

On the evening of the 2nd of July there came an order to be in readiness to march at a moment's notice. We packed up all our belongings tents and all else and sat around or lay upon the ground expecting every moment to be ordered into ranks. For the rest of the night we lay upon our faces and slept. Many times the rattling of the sabers of passing cavalry or the rumbling of artillery with their heavy guns would awaken me.

– *Chauncey Cooke, 25th Infantry, Wisconsin*

I made my way over the bridge and lay down on a beautiful sand bar by the river. I fell asleep, and for a time forgot I was a soldier on a battlefield. Very early in the morning I was aroused by the familiar boom of cannon and rattle of musketry. I was nearly frozen, for the damp sand had chilled me through.

- J. W. Reid

Fifteen-inch gun used in the defense of Washington, D.C.

FRONT LINES

Morris Island (vicinity), South Carolina
Confederate lines west of Atlanta

The "Marsh Battery" or "Swamp Angel"
after the explosion, August 22, 1863

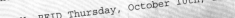

Our regiment is again on picket guard. I will now try
to explain to you how our different guards are arranged
so that you can understand it. In the first place we
have what we call a regimental guard (every regiment
has one). So many men are detailed every morning from
each company, and are posted around the regiment to
watch for the enemy and to see that everything is going
on right. This guard is divided into three reliefs,
one relief on post at a time, being relieved every two
hours, so that each relief is on post just one-third of
the time. We also have what we call a brigade guard.
Men are detailed from the regiments constituting a
brigade, and a portion of them are placed on all the
roads and highways leading toward our camps, divided
into reliefs, as the regimental guard.

-J. W. REID Thursday, October 10th, 1861

Above and left: Views of Confederate fort near Atlanta

64-pounder confederate gun at Yorktown, Virginia, which burst in the effort to reach Federal siege guns

Lieutenant Commmander Edward Barrett and Lieutenant Cornelius N. Schoonmaker of the U.S. monitor, Sullivan's Island, South Carolina

Confederate fortifications with quaker (wooden logs) guns in foreground, winter barracks in background

Exploded gun in Confederate battery, Yorktown, Virginia

FRONT LINES

Top left: Captain Perkins's "Secesh" horse captured at Cornwallis cave

Bottom right: Confederate fortifications near Atlanta

Interior view of Castle Pinckney, Charleston, South Carolina

Bomb-proof shelter for telegraph operator on Morris Island, South Carolina

LEE'S MEN   **CONFEDERATE**

The faces of the veterans in this photograph of 1864 reflect more forcibly than volumes of historical essays, the privations and the courage of the ragged veterans in gray who faced Grant, with Lee as their leader. They did not know that their struggle had already become unavailing; that no amount of perseverance and devotion could make headway against the resources, determination, and discipline of the Northern armies, now that they had become concentrated and wielded by a master of men like Grant. But Grant was as yet little more than a name to the armies of the East. His successes had been won on Western fields—Donelson, Vicksburg, Chattanooga. It was not yet known that the Army of the Potomac under the new general-in-chief was to prove irresistible. So these faces reflect perfect confidence

Though prisoners when this picture was t[...] June, when he sent some ten thousand Con[...] stroke against Lee—though their arms have [...] "uniform," their hats partly the regulation [...] caps, and partly nondescript—yet these m[...] ment. To them, "Marse Robert" is still [...] and again have held their own, and more; t[...] assault, however impossible it seems, knowi[...]

Lee's men

Top: Cooks in the kitchen of Soldiers' Rest in Vicksburg, Virginia

Bottom: Snowball battle near Dalton, Georgia

RS IN VIRGINIA, 1864

nant of Grant's heavy captures during May and
Coxey's Landing, Virginia, as a result of his first
from them, though their uniforms are anything but
Army of Northern Virginia, partly captured Federal
ans stand and sit with the dignity of accomplish-
unconquerable, under whom inferior numbers again
leader under whom every man gladly rushes to any
y order will be made to count.

FRONT LINES

Above: Horse artillery on parade grounds

Right: Nick Biddle, the first man wounded in the War Between the States

Facing page: Unidentified young soldier in Confederate shell jacket and forage cap with single shot pistol

"NICK BIDDLE,"
Of Pottsville, Pa. the first man wounded in the Great
American Rebellion, "Baltimore, April 18, 1861."

Sherman, leaning on breach of gun, outside Atlanta

The "Wizard" cannon

Parrot rifle after bursting of muzzle

Bronze Indian cannon, 17th century. Bannerman's

English hand mortar, late 16th century. Ancient Armor

Phillipine cannons, 19th century. Bannerman's

Sixteenth century serpentine, drawn by Albrecht Durer. Century Dictionary

Fifteenth century cannons. Sunday Book

Charleston harbor battery during the Civil War. Harper's

Display of field artillery

PROFESSOR LOWE'S BALLOON "EAGLE" IN A STORM.

Top: *Professor Lowe's balloon Eagle in a storm*

Bottom: *Confederate naval battery at Yorktown, Virginia; Nelson Church hospital (in background)*

Top: Bringing Parrott gun into position on board gunboat Mendota

Left: Sling for transporting big guns

Removing munitions from captured fort

Artillery battalion

Wharves after the explosion of ordnance barges on August 4, 1864, City Point, Virginia

I think it was on the night of the 23d of January, 1865, that an attempt was made to get the iron-clads down the river, the object being to destroy General Grant's transports and stores at City Point. Had this succeeded it would have made a very great difference in the result of the next campaign. City Point was the base of General Grant's supplies, and if they had been destroyed, and we had resumed the control of the river, it is difficult to say what would have become of his army. It might have led to his surrender, and in any event would have seriously crippled him.
– Recollections of a Naval Officer, Edwin H. Brigham, M. D.

Captain Joseph Banks Lyle, C.S.A., 5th Infantry South Carolina, who single-handedly captured more than 500 Union soldiers.

Grounded Confederate torpedo boat in Charleston, South Carolina

Major General Prince Polignac, a French aristocrat, who served in the Confederate Army.

Camp of Confederate soldiers at Belle Plain, Virginia

U.S.S. Steam Sloop of War, with 18 guns

The Robert E. Lee I and the Great Republic at the wharf

Confederate soldiers stealing supplies from Union forces

"MERRIMAC" IN DRY DOCK, BEING CONVERTED INTO
THE IRON BATTERY "VIRGINIA."

*The transport Black Hawk —damaged
after Red River Expedition*

Gunboat Commodore McDonough

Professor Lowe's military balloon near Gaines Mill, Virginia

Top: *The Rattler—leader of the "Land Cruise" in 1863*

Left: *Integrated Union naval crew*

Bottom: *A besieging "tinclad"—the Marmora*

A BESIEGING "TINCLAD"—THE "MARMORA"

Butler's dredge-boat, sunk by a Confederate shell

FRONT LINES

The sack of the Blair Mansion

Below: Confederate playing card

Muskets used as a coatrack

Camp Cameron

Left: Lieutenants George A. Custer, Nicolas Bowen and William G. Jones

Bottom: Cockfighting at General Wilcox's headquarters

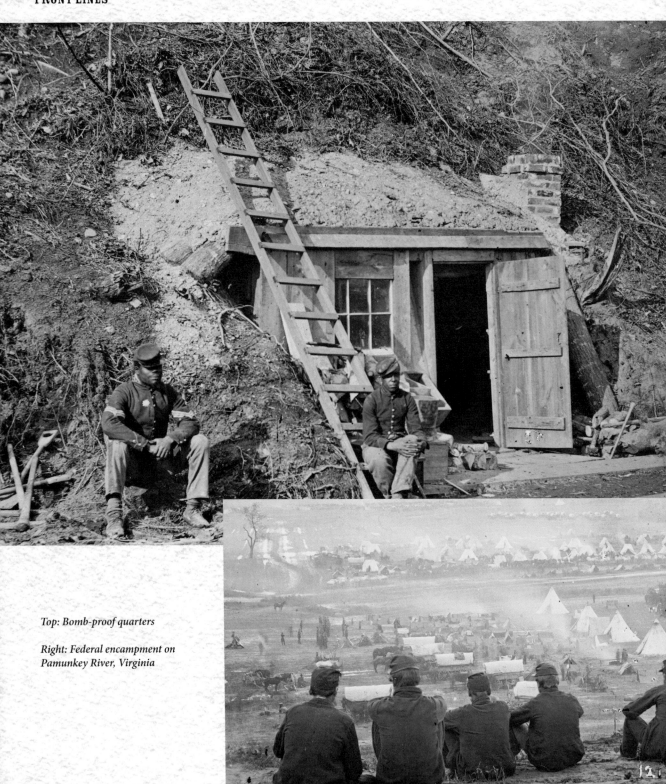

Top: Bomb-proof quarters

Right: Federal encampment on Pamunkey River, Virginia

On guard, father and son

General William F. Bartlett and staff
Washington, D.C. (vicinity)

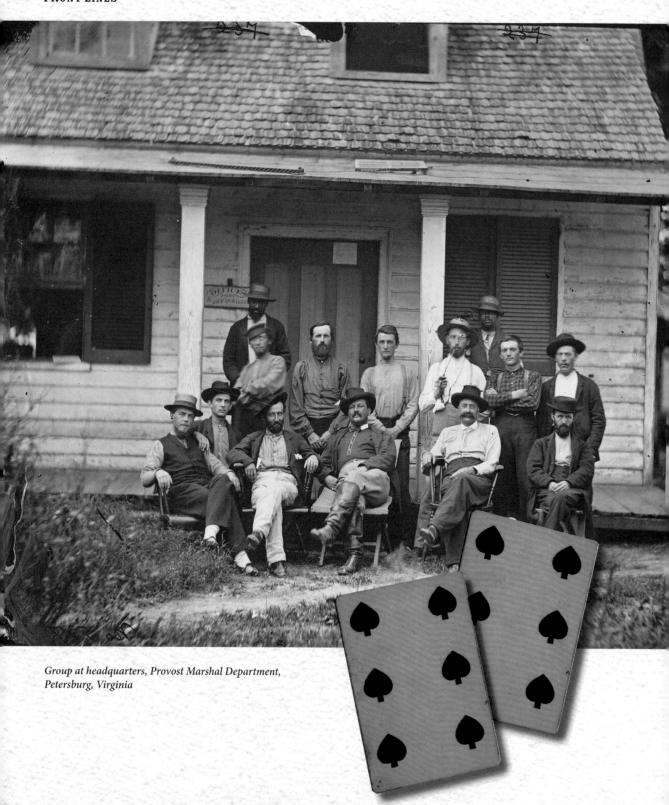

Group at headquarters, Provost Marshal Department,
Petersburg, Virginia

Above and left: On skirmish line

Above: African Americans on horseback leaving fields to join Union troops marching in background.

Below: Carrying the powder down the covered way to the mine under fire

REGULATIONS FOR CAMP DEFIANCE

Reveille at	5
Breakfast Call at	7
Guard Mounting at	9½
Dinner Call at	12
Company Drills from	1 to 3
Dress Parade at	6
Tattoo at	9
Taps at	10

1. All non-commissioned Officers will be within the Camp at 8 P. M.
2. No commissioned Officer will be allowed to remain out of the Camp after Tattoo, without the permission of his Battalion Commander.
3. After 8 P. M. no loud singing, no cheering or firing arms will be allowed, nor any firing or cheering on the Sabbath. The Commandant requests that the troops will observe the Sabbath in an orderly and Christian-like manner.
4. Citizens visiting the Camp must obtain a written pass from Head Quarters.
5. Guards, when recognizing Staff Officers and commissioned Officers of the line, will pass them, in the daylight, without the countersign.

The Commandant will hold the various commanders strictly accountable to the observance of the above.

By order of   B. M. PRENTISS, Commandant.

CHICAGO HISTORICAL SOCIETY

AN ACT

Recognizing the existence of War between the United States and the Confederate States; and concerning letters of marque, prizes, and prize goods.

WHEREAS, the earnest efforts made by this Government to establish friendly relations between the Government of the United States and the Confederate States, and to settle all questions of disagreement between the two Governments upon principles of right, justice, equity and good faith, have proved unavailing by reason of the refusal of the Government of the United States to hold any intercourse with the Commissioners appointed by this Government for the purposes aforesaid, or to listen to any proposals they had to make for the peaceful solution of all causes of difficulty between the two Governments; and whereas the President of the United States of America has issued his proclamation making requisition upon the States of the American Union for seventy-five thousand men for the purpose, as therein indicated, of capturing forts and other strong-holds within the jurisdiction of and belonging to the Confederate States of America, and has detailed naval armaments upon the coasts of the Confederate States of America, and raised, organised and equipped a large military force to execute the purpose aforesaid, and has issued his other proclamation announcing his purpose to set on foot a blockade of the ports of the Confederate States: and whereas the State of Virginia has seceded from the Federal Union and entered into a convention of alliance offensive and defensive with the Confederate States, and has adopted the Provisional Constitution of the said States, and the States of Maryland, North Carolina, Tennessee, Kentucky, Arkansas and Missouri, have refused, and it is believed that the State of Delaware and the inhabitants of the Territories of Arizona and New Mexico, and the Indian Territory South of Kansas, will refuse to co-operate with the Government of the United States in these acts of hostilities and wanton aggression, which are plainly intended to over-awe, oppress, and finally subjugate the people of the Confederate States; and whereas, by the acts and means aforesaid, war exists between the Confederate States and the Government of the United States, and the States and Territories thereof, except the States of Maryland, North Carolina, Tennessee, Kentucky, Arkansas, Missouri and Delaware, and the Territories of Arizona and New Mexico, and the Indian Territory South of Kansas: Therefore

SEC. 1. *The Congress of the Confederate States of America do enact*, That the President of the Confede-

rate States is hereby authorized to use the whole land and naval force of the Confederate States to meet the war thus commenced, and to issue to private armed vessels commissions, or _____ reprisal, in such form _____ the seal of the Confede _____ goods, and effects of _____ States, and of the citiz _____ and Territories thereo _____ perty of the enemy (_____ laden on board a neut _____ seizure under this a _____ vessels of the citize _____ States now in the p _____ cept such as have b _____ may hereafter be in _____ the United States, _____ the publication of _____ reach their destina _____ goes, excepting _____ be subject to capt _____ od, unless they sh _____ nation for which _____ ports.

SEC. 2. That _____ shall be and he _____ revoke and ann _____ reprisal which _____ this act.

SEC. 3. Th _____ marque and r _____ writing the _____ tonnage and _____ of residence _____ intended nu _____ be signed by the person or perso _____ cation, and filed with the Secretary of State, or shall be delivered to any other officer or person who shall be employed to deliver out such commissions, to be by him transmitted to the Secretary of State.

SEC. 4. That before any commission or letters of marque and reprisal shall be issued as aforesaid, the owner or owners of the ship or vessel for which the same shall be requested, and the commander thereof for the time being, shall give bond to the Confederate States, with at least two responsible sureties, not inter-

Dead Confederate soldier

View of Knoxville from Fort Stanley

View of Atlanta before it was burned. This photograph was requested by General Sherman.

Lieutenant Robert Clarke, Captain John C. Tidball, Lieutenant William N. Dennison, and Captain Alexander C.M. Pennington

FRONT LINES

A. Greenwall, Confederate Army officer

Cook stove on U.S.S. Monitor

Columbiad guns of the Confederate water battery

General A.J. Vaughn, of Texas, C.S.A.

Micah Jenkins, Brigadier General, C.S.A.

15 Confederate Artillery, Loading.

Photograph of Confederate artillery loading, near Charleston, South Carolina

FRONT LINES

New Hampshire 3rd Infantry, Company A

Major General George Meade with corps commanders

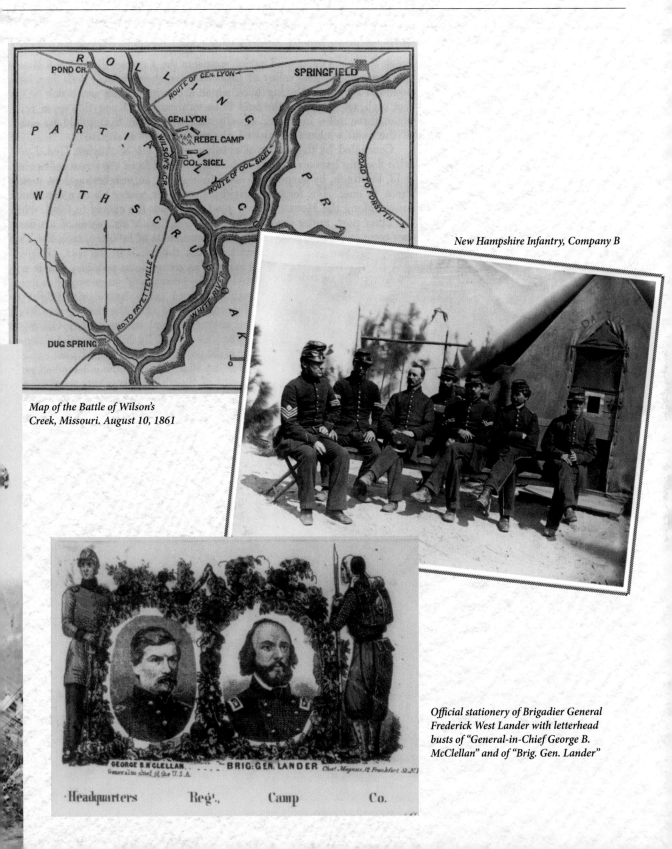

Map of the Battle of Wilson's Creek, Missouri. August 10, 1861

New Hampshire Infantry, Company B

Official stationery of Brigadier General Frederick West Lander with letterhead busts of "General-in-Chief George B. McClellan" and of "Brig. Gen. Lander"

Bodies of Confederate dead gathered for burial, Antietam, Maryland

Lincoln's Gettysburg Address, Gettysburg, Pennsylvania

BATTLES

†

MANY BRAVE MEN

As I reached the brow of the hill back of Falmouth I could see the rebel camp fires all along the side of the hill beyond Fredericksburg, where also those terrible batteries are placed which cut our armies to pieces at the late battle, and which many of our men consider almost impregnable. Our regiment lost 4 killed and 12 wounded. Our company lost none, but Henry Caryl came very near being wounded, a spent ball striking his arm but not breaking the skin.

Delavan Bates, 121st Infantry, New York

The Yankees seem loath to make another advance since the good whipping we gave them here on the thirteenth in the battle of Fredericksburg. Milton Bossardt's company went into the fight with forty men, and thirty of them were killed or wounded. He escaped very narrowly. A hole was shot through his hat and one of his shoe heels was shot off. Pick Stevens never shuns a fight. He goes boldly into them all.

Letter from Spencer Glasgow Welch, 13th Infantry, South Carolina

Sentry ovelooking Tennessee Valley

The Baggage Guard

Top left: The Battle of Pittsburgh, Tennessee

Middle left: The Rebel raid at Garlick's Landing, Pamunkey River, Virginia

Bottom right: Battle of Savage's Station, Virginia

RUNNING AMMUNITION TRAINS INTO THE CHICK

Running ammunition trains into the Chickahominy

A little after daylight they appeared in large numbers and soon attacked. We held our ground as long as possible, giving them as good as they sent, until about 7 o'clock, when they came in such overwhelming numbers as to force us back on our main lines, a distance of about six hundred yards, with the loss of several of our men. I lost all my clothing and blankets. In falling back we had a slanting hill to go down and when we got to the foot of it our artillery opened fire on the enemy over our heads, this stopped them from following us. We then took a circuitous route, so as not to be in the way of the artillery, finally got around and went into the fort, near the main road to Williamsburg. While skirmishing that morning we left several men killed or wounded, who fell into the enemy's hands. While Thomas Stacks and another man were carrying off Archibald Sadler, who was wounded, the man who was helping was shot dead and a Minnie ball struck Stack's canteen and tore it all to pieces. Stacks left Sadler, and he is now in the enemy's hands. He is badly wounded. A ball went through my overcoat, but did not graze the skin.

About the time that brigade made its unsuccessful charge night came on and ended the slaughter.

Yours as ever, J. W. REID

Lee to the rear, Spottsylvania, May 13, 1864

BOMBARDMENT AND CAPTURE OF FREDERICKSBURG, VA. DEC. 11TH 1862.

BY THE ARMY OF THE POTOMAC, UNDER GEN! BURNSIDE.

At sunrise ... opened on the City with 143 pieces of Artillery and set it on fire in several places. The attempt was then made to complete the pontoon bridge across the Rappahannock, but the rebel sharpshooters drove us back. Volunteers were then called for, to cross the river in small boats and dislodge the enemy; thousands sprang out of the ranks, but only a hundred were accepted, who crossed the river in the most dashing style, drove back the sharpshooters at the point of the bayonet, and captured over a hundred of them. The bridges were then completed and the army crossed in safety.

Right: Officers on deck of a Union monitor warship

CHARGE OF IRWIN'S BRIGADE AT THE DUNKER CHURCH. (BY EDWIN FORBES, AFTER HIS SKETCH MADE AT THE TIME.)

General Wm. F. Smith, commanding the Second Division of Franklin's corps, went to the assistance of French. On getting into position, for the most part to the right of French, General Smith, in his report, says: "Finding that the enemy were advancing, I ordered forward the Third Brigade (Colonel Irwin's), who, passing through the regular battery then commanded by Lieutenant Thomas (Fourth Artillery), charged upon the enemy and drove them gallantly until abreast the little church at the point of woods, the possession of which had been so fiercely contested. At this point a severe flank fire from the woods was received." The brigade rallied behind the crest of a slope, and remained in an advanced position until the next day.— EDITOR.

CAMP NEAR RICHMOND, VIRGINIA, June 2, 1862

The sulphur and smoke o'ershadowed the earth, And the cannon they did rattle, And many brave men lie cold in the earth, Who were slain in Seven Pines battle.

We marched through a pine thicket, along a big road, and then through an old field, and right in front of us was a battery of nine cannon, supported by a considerable force of infantry. They were but a few hundred yards in advance of us, and immediately opened fire. Our numbers being so small we made a flank movement to our left, making for a thick piece of woods that was but a short distance away, as we thought we would be sheltered from the storm of ball and shell which played havoc in our ranks.

View off Antietam battlefield

The other companies of the battalion, what was left of them, remained, and we did what shooting we could while laying on the ground amongst our dead and wounded comrades. It was but a short time before the expected reinforcement joined us, when we drove the enemy out of the woods with considerable loss on their side. By this side the fighting became hot on both sides and in the centre, Longstreet's position, as usual. I cannot convey an idea of the terrors of the next few hours. As I said at the beginning of this letter. The sulphur and smoke o'ershadowed the earth, And the cannon they did rattle.

Yours as ever, J. W. REID

Drilling troops near Washington, D.C.

Sic semper tyrannis - 22th Regiment U.S. Colored Troops

RICHMOND, VIRGINIA, May 29, 1862
A battle with ten or twenty thousand men engaged is called a skirmish.
We read and boast of the great battles fought by Washington and others.
Washington never had more than fifteen or twenty thousand men with him at
any one time, and never fought as big a battle as that of Williamsburg,
the other day, and that was a skirmish compared to the one now pending.
The armies will be counted by hundreds of thousands. I apprehend that
before this letter ends there will be more men killed than Washington or
Lord Cornwallis had in their combined armies.

Yours as ever, J. W. REID.

Major General John Alexander Logan and staff in Vicksburg

Edward Ferrero, Colonel

Benjamin Franklin Fisher, Captain

George Stoneman, Union General

TO PATIENCE WALKER

Galitan, Tennessee
November the 12th, 1862
Dear Mother, —
I take this opportunity of writing to you to let you know that I am well and hope
that these few lines may find you and the rest of them well.
We have crossed over the Kentucky line and have gone over into Tennessee twenty-five
miles. It is a very nice place here and it is not cold either. It is about as warm
here now as it is in September in Ohio.
The 31st Ohio regiment is within a mile and a half of here but I. have not seen
any of them and don't expect to, for we are not through traveling yet. We expect to
leave here this afternoon or tomorrow and go to Lebanon, Tennessee. I do not know
when we will stop to stay any time nor don't care much, for I have gotten so used to
traveling that it does not tire me.
I have not gotten any letters from any of the folks for about two weeks. I must
close and march.
This is from your son,
Robert Walker

GEN. JOHN H. MORGAN AND STAFF.—Engraved by W. B. Campbell.

CAPTURE OF FORT DONELSON, T

Capture of Fort Donelson, Tennessee, Charge of General Smith's division

Tripod signal

General Osterhaus

The demand for the surrender of New Orleans

General Lee on horseback

Scouts and guides for the Army of the Potomac, Berlin Maryland 1862

Fed observation balloon being inflated
Battle of Fair Oaks, 1862

The Naval Attack on Forts Jackson and St Philip, New Orl
copied from a painting belonging to Admiral Porter

Naval attack of Forts Jackson and St. Phillip, New Orleans

Battle of Lexington, Mississippi

Hilton Head South Carolina 1862 New Hampshire Infantry

TO HARRIET WALKER

Lebanon, Tennessee

November the 13th, 1862
Dear Sister, —

I take this opportunity of writing
to let you know that I am well and
hope that these few lines may find
you enjoying the same blessing.

We get plenty to eat, such as
beans, rice, meat, coffee,
crackers and chicken. We buy our
chicken with the Southern scrip.
I have ten dollars of it yet,
and some good money about four
dollars. But my stamps have run
out and I can't get any more.

No more at present.Write soon and
tell the rest to write. Then I
will.

ROBERT WALKER

Camp of 3rd New Hampshire Infantry, Hilton Head South Carolina February 28, 1862

BATTLES   †   MANY BRAVE MEN

*Long Bridge over the Potomac; Union troops
guarding against infiltration by Confederate spies*

Memphis Commercial Appeal

A part of the 5th Ohio regiment of the Union army, entering Memphis on June 6, 1862.

Engraving showing the Confederate flag against night sky with moon and stars. Surrounding smaller scenes include "A charge in the wilderness," "The crater," "The fight in Hampton Roads," and "After the surrender."

Published by the Sherman Publishing Co. New York.

FAMOUS UNION COMMANDERS OF THE CIVIL W

GEN. GEO. H. THOMAS.   GEN. PHILIP KEARNEY.   GEN. A. E. BURNSIDE.   GEN. JOSEPH HOOKER.   GEN. JOHN A. LOGAN.
GEN. IRWIN McDOWELL.   GEN. N. P. BANKS.   GEN. PHILIP H. SHERIDAN.   GEN. U. S. GRANT.   GEN. W. T. SHERMAN.
ADMIRAL DAVID G. FARRAGUT.   GEN. JOHN POPE.   GEN. BENJAMIN F. BUTLER.   GEN. WINFIELD S. HANCOCK.

This, and a Companion Engraving, representing TWENTY [20] FAMOUS CONFEDERATE COMMANDERS, given as PREMIUMS to Subscribers to the Book "The Pictorial Battles of the Civil

61-'65.

GEN. GEO. B. McCLELLAN,
GEN. DANIEL E. SICKLES,
ADMIRAL DAVID D. PORTER.

Sherman Publishing Co., New York.

MICROFILMED

Copyrighted 1884 by the Sherman Publishing Co. New York.

TO HARRIET WALKER

Camp Seven Miles from Nashville, Tennessee
Sunday, November 23, 1862
Dear Sister, —

I take this opportunity to write you a few lines to let you know that I have not forgotten to write, if you have. I have not gotten a letter from you for a coon's age. I think that as much news as there is in Saltlick township, you could find something to write about.

I know of some of the news, such as weddings. I heard of Joseph Harrison and Luvina Moore being married, and Triscy Petit and Noah Cofman.

And I heard about that poor unfortunate girl, Mary Campfield, getting her leg broken. I should like to know who she blames for the mischief.

I heard that Nathan Buchanan had gotten his discharge. I want to know if he is sick and how he is getting along. I suppose that you girls have big times with him and James Turner, and Nelson and George Spurrier, for that is all of the boys whom you have in our district.

I think that you ought to have a party occasionally — a play or sprucing party. You girls can have your parties to yourselves this fall, and next fall I think that the soldiers will get home. Then we shall have our parties to ourselves and we won't have any girls to them.
When you write, I want you to tell me what kind of times you have, who is teaching our school, and what Ball's girls and Wests are doing. Tell Spurrier's boys that if they want me to write to them, they must write to me first, for I have written to both of them and got no answer.
You said that you wanted me to get my likeness taken, if it did not cost too much. There is no chance at all here. Write as soon as this comes to hand and write all the news. Cut some good pieces out of the newspaper and send. Next time I shall write more.

Good-bye.
ROBERT WALKER

EXTERIOR VIEW

INTERIOR VIEW OF THE
COOPER SHOP VOLUNTEER REFRESHMENT SALOON,
THE FIRST OPENED FOR UNION VOLUNTEERS IN THE UNITED STATES.
1009 Otsego St.   PHILADELPHIA.

W.B. Hatch, Colonel 4th New Jersey Infantry

Reverend Dr. Clifford H. Plumer, Clergy

J. Albert Monroe, Lieutenant Colonel, Rhode Island Artillery

Ulysses S. Grant, with cigar in his mouth, on horseback

Grant, from West Point to Appomattox

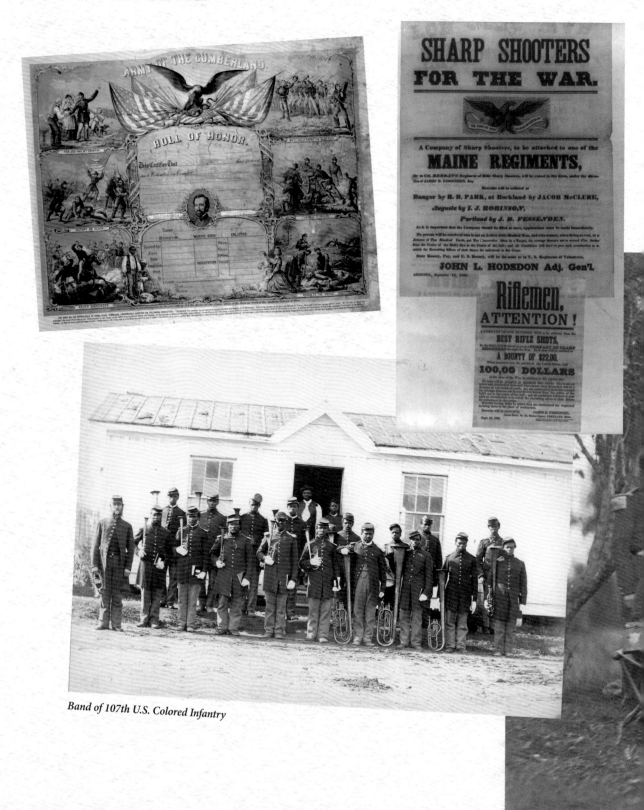

Band of 107th U.S. Colored Infantry

Left: Band of the 10th Veteran Reserve Corps

Bottom: Elmira Cornet Band

BEHIND THE SCENES

Esteemed Sir: I have arrived from Hamburg general hospital. I have 160 of the sick under my care. They are doing quite as well as we could hope for under the circumstances—have lost none, have nurses plenty, but nee good cooks. This is the mistake. Good cooks are what is most needed in our hospitals. Fruits, potatoes, onions, barley, whisky and lots of peppers are needed too.

- Mr. E. Russell, Cor. Secretary Scott Co. Relief Association

I am now clerking at the Variola Hospital. Everything was so much out of order that I had a good deal of work to get straightened up. I have got everything to working right now, and have some leisure. I am now living in a tent. The office has had so many smallpox clothes in it that I preferred a tent. I am getting used to camp life. The tent is keeping up a lively flapping today. It is very blustery. The tent floor is shaking so I can scarcely write.

- W.O. Ruddock (23rd Infantry, North Carolina)

Confederate hospital near Richmond, Virginia

BEHIND THE SCENES

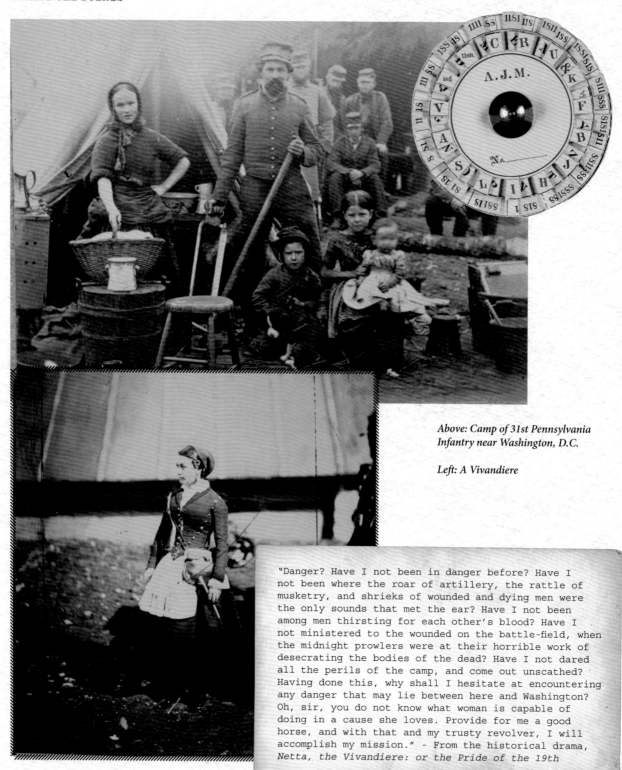

Above: Camp of 31st Pennsylvania Infantry near Washington, D.C.

Left: A Vivandiere

"Danger? Have I not been in danger before? Have I not been where the roar of artillery, the rattle of musketry, and shrieks of wounded and dying men were the only sounds that met the ear? Have I not been among men thirsting for each other's blood? Have I not ministered to the wounded on the battle-field, when the midnight prowlers were at their horrible work of desecrating the bodies of the dead? Have I not dared all the perils of the camp, and come out unscathed? Having done this, why shall I hesitate at encountering any danger that may lie between here and Washington? Oh, sir, you do not know what woman is capable of doing in a cause she loves. Provide for me a good horse, and with that and my trusty revolver, I will accomplish my mission." - From the historical drama, *Netta, the Vivandiere: or the Pride of the 19th*

Tending a horse

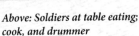

*Above: Soldiers at table eating;
cook, and drummer*

Left: Walt Whitman

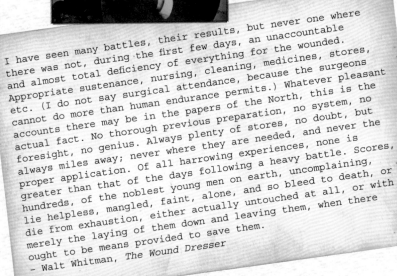

I have seen many battles, their results, but never one where
there was not, during the first few days, an unaccountable
and almost total deficiency of everything for the wounded.
Appropriate sustenance, nursing, cleaning, medicines, stores,
etc. (I do not say surgical attendance, because the surgeons
cannot do more than human endurance permits.) Whatever pleasant
accounts there may be in the papers of the North, this is the
actual fact. No thorough previous preparation, no system, no
foresight, no genius. Always plenty of stores, no doubt, but
always miles away; never where they are needed, and never the
proper application. Of all harrowing experiences, none is
greater than that of the days following a heavy battle. Scores,
hundreds, of the noblest young men on earth, uncomplaining,
lie helpless, mangled, faint, alone, and so bleed to death, or
die from exhaustion, either actually untouched at all, or with
merely the laying of them down and leaving them, when there
ought to be means provided to save them.
– Walt Whitman, *The Wound Dresser*

Above: Brother Jonathan, armed with many weapons; with inscription: "South's the word, and South I'm going! Hurrah for the Star Spangled Banner! The Union must and shall be preserved! Our war cry is death to Traitors! God bless our country!"

Left: Captain Sellers and wife at Fort Totten

BEHIND THE SCENE

Two women trimming a soldier's hair

Government repair shops

PHILAD-
N.Y. AND
BALTIMORE
PAPERS.

Marriage in a camp

Scouts and guides, Army of the Potomac

Burial of soldier

Union blacksmith shop

Constructing road on south bank of North Anna River

B-5077

Above: View of destroyed gun carriage in second traverse,
Fort Fisher, North Carolina
Left: Mathew Brady's photography outfit in the field.

July 5th 1862
Camp Lincoln, James River

Friend Paul,

I was down with an attack of the bilious & remittent fever, brought on by exposure to the damned climate in the cursed swamps. For a month I could scarcely crawl dosed with mercury & whiskey till I have learned to hate that fluid and cannot smoke without nausea. However I am well and almost as strong as before, in which I am lucky, as numbers of the soldiers have died of the same fever. To tell you the truth, no amount of money can pay a man for going through what we have had to suffer lately, and being, to my great astonishment alive, I feel a good deal like leaving myself.

The government by wickedly withholding the reinforcements, which little Mac [General McClellan] has required for two months, has almost caused the annihilation of this army. The enemy almost surrounded us two or three to one on this Chickahominy and the only chance left us was to fight our way to the James River and the protection of our gunboats. For seven days against immense odds this gallant army has fought like heroes, covering the retreat of the baggage trains, and rolling back the devilish grey coats, in every attack. Only think of it, seven days almost without food or sleep, night and day being attacked by overwhelming mapes of infuriate rebels, thundering at us from all sides, and finally securing our position, utterly worn out, in a drenching rain, with a loss of nearly 35000 men, 80 pieces of artillery and 300 wagons destroyed to keep them out of the enemies hands. So dogged have our men fought that the enemies loss foots up to a much higher figure than ours. At the last day's fight, they made sure they had us, but with such fury did our soldiers stand at bay, that 10,000 of the rebels fell and our loss was but 1000. Where the rebels lay, the ground looked like a burnt forest so thickly the grey bodies covered the ground.

I think we shall stay here-30 miles below Richmond-for some time. I do not think we have more than 60000 men, and it must be 150000, before we can take the offensive again. I envy you your quiet jog, plenty to eat and drink and no risk from damned shells and bullets. I heard Nast was with you. Between you and I, I detest him. Give my remembrance to all friends, I have been told Sol is down upon me, I never meant to give him offence, and do not understand how I have - however, can't stop for that as we say in the army.

When I write this, the woods where the enemy is ensconced are in full view separated from our position by corn and wheat fields, all along our line I see batteries in position ready to repel any attack. Franklin's balloon is up in the air watching the rebs, and the advance camps of the infantry dot the fields with their little shelter tents. Our army is in excellent spirits, and the bands, not allowed to play before Richmond, are in full blast again & are at work. Infantry reliefs going out a picket, or to cut down the woods, to form batteries in front, strings of artillery horses going to water, mean building houses for shade cooking progressing in all directions, wagons moving up and down from the river with commissary stores for the soldiers, everything orderly and shipshape again.

On the river the gunboats lay sleepily watching the enemy on the opposite shore and our flank fleets of transports, and hospital steamers, covered with flags make quite a gay scene, and confidence is engendered in the minds of all. The rebels are evidently afraid to attack us, and the longer they wait, the worse it will be for them with which sentiment I conclude and subscribe myself

Sincerely your friend,
Alfred Waud

1st Virginia Cavalry at a halt

Alfred Waud, who was recognized as the best sketch artist of the Civil War

BEHIND THE SCENES

Facing page: General Ambrose E. Burnside (reading newspaper) with Mathew B. Brady (nearest tree) at Army of the Potomac headquarters

Above: Theodore Russell Davis, sketch artist for Harper's Weekly

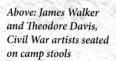

Above: James Walker and Theodore Davis, Civil War artists seated on camp stools

Right: Photographer Timothy O'Sullivan at Manassas

Bridge at Strawberry Plains, near Knoxville, Tennessee

Engine Commodore lying on its side near Brandy Station, Virginia

Picnic party at Antietam bridge

BEHIND THE SCENES

Dear Sister H. —

It is Saturday night, and I am sitting in one of my pleasantest rooms, watching over several of my boys. You can have no idea of their suffering, even if I should attempt to describe it. In the next room are two handsome young men, unconscious of suffering, who have been dying all night, and we are ignorant about their friends, as they came to us so delirious that they knew nothing. We always get their names if possible when the ambulance brings them in, that we may telegraph to their friends. When they are brought in they are carried to the bath room, stripped entirely and washed thoroughly; then they are put into bed and the clothing they wore is rolled up, after the money, photographs and the like are taken from their pockets, their name marked on their bundle, then, with the sword and knapsack, it is put in a shed, on a shelf, until called for. Many of our patients are dying of typhoid. Their tongues are black and their breath is extremely offensive.

While I am writing, a New York company is doing escort duty for one who was a patient of mine, who is to be buried tomorrow. As many of my boys ask me the name of their dead mates, I take the opportunity to speak to them of their need of preparation for the same change, and they always listen with great attention. I have become familiar with death. Often I am called at the solemn hour of mid- night to stand alone by the bedside of the dying, and close mouth and eyes. Many have died clasping my hand tightly. O, dear sister, will you ask every friend of mine to pray for the dying soldier? The prayers he utters for wife or mother are often heart-rending, but I cannot talk to him, for his ears are past all sound. I feel that I am placed in a very trying situation. How could I do what I am called to if I was not strengthened by an unseen hand and fed daily and hourly with the bread of heaven?

From a letter by Rebecca R. Pomroy in *Echoes of the War*

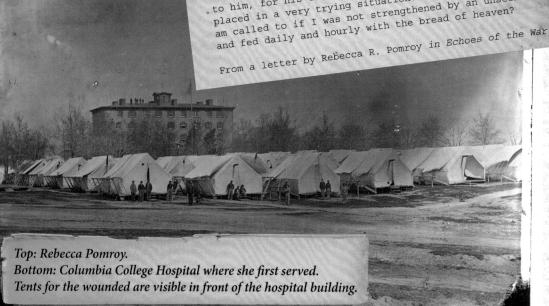

Top: Rebecca Pomroy.
Bottom: Columbia College Hospital where she first served.
Tents for the wounded are visible in front of the hospital building.

Above: U.S. Christian Commission which provided social services to Union soldiers

Right: Portion of a speech by Clara Barton, Clara Barton, the leader of the effort to bring hospital supplies to the battlefield, above

BEHIND THE SCENES

UNION HOSPITAL IN A BARN NEAR ANTIETAM CREEK. (BY EDWIN FORBES, AFTER HIS SKETCH MADE AT THE TIME.)

Union Hospital at Antietam

Embalming surgeon at work on soldier's body

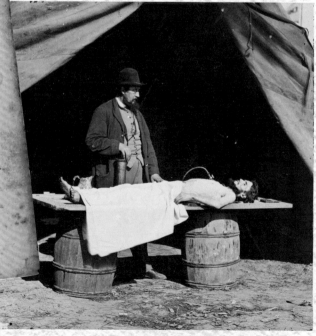

June 27th, 1864

When our division was withdrawn from the extreme front, where it has been since the beginning of the campaign, we surgeons looked for a little less arduous work; but now the artillery brigade has been placed under our care, and we have as much to do as ever.

It has not rained for a month, and the poor wounded fellows lie all about me, suffering intensely from heat and flies. The atmosphere is almost intolerable from the immense quantity of decomposing animal and vegetable matter upon the ground. Many of the surgeons are ill, and I indulge in large doses of quinine. Horses and mules die by hundreds from continued hard labor and scant feed. The roads are strewn with them, and the decay of these, with that of human bodies in the trenches, causes malaria of the worst kind.

War! war! war! I often think that in the future, when human character shall have deepened, there will be a better way of settling affairs than this of plunging into a perfect maelstrom of horror.

John Perry Gardner
Massachusetts Infantry, 20th Regiment

Above and below: Straw huts erected on Smith's farm used as a hospital after the battle of Antietam, Keedysville, Maryland (vicinity)

Dear father and mother,

I am now in Washington at the Hospital sick and should like to see you very much and should like to have you come and see me. I do not weigh more than 100 pounds now. I came with Mr. Morse of Plymouth and did not know it until we had been out a spell. I think that if it had not been for him I should have starved to death because the Doctor did not take any care of the sick at all aboard of the boat.

From your son,
Ansel J. Bartlett, 58th Mass Vols

Above: Orphaned boys of Civil War soldiers

Below: Civil War surgeon Mary E. Walker

Left: Amputation being performed in a mobile hospital

BEHIND THE SCENES

Hospital attendants collecting the wounded near Hatcher's Run, Virginia

Hospital train interior

Confederate field hospital near Cedar Mountain, Virginia

Naval hospital

Wounded from the Battle of the Wilderness, Virginia

BATTLES

✝

DETERMINED TO WIN

We came in sight of the enemy when we had advanced a few yards, and were saluted with cannon. We pushed on, however, to the old railroad cut, in which most of Jackson's troops lay. The troops occupying this place had expended their ammunition and were defending themselves with rocks...which seemed to have been picked or blasted out of the bed of the railroad, chips and slivers of stone which many were collecting and others were throwing.

– Lieutenant Robert Healey, 27th Indiana

As my brigade advanced through the woods to retake the position, the minnie balls were rattling like hail against the trees, and as we debouched into the field through which the railroad cut ran, nothing could be seen between us and the smoke and fire of the enemy's rifles except the tattered battle flag of the Louisiana brigade; the staff of this was stuck in the ground at the edge of the cut, and the brigade was at the bottom of it throwing stones.

- Robert M. Mayo, 47th Virginia Infantry

STARKE'S LOUISIANA BRIGADE FIGHTING WITH STONES AT THE EMBANKMENT NEAR THE "DEEP CUT."

Battle-field of the Wildern[...]

Distant view of Lacy Hous[...]
from Old Wilderness Taver[...]

Battle of Chickamauga, Georgia

THE REBELS RETREATING WITH THEIR PLUNDER ACROSS THE POTOMAC RIVER.

"The Rebels Retreating with their Plunder Across the Potomac River"

But in the middle of September Longstreet came to Bragg's rescue; and a desperate battle was fought at Chickamauga on the nineteenth and twentieth. The Confederates had seventy thousand men against fifty-six thousand Federals: odds of five to four. They were determined to win at any price; and it cost them eighteen thousand men, killed, wounded, and missing; which was two thousand more than the Federals lost. But they felt it was now or never as they turned to bay with, for once, superior numbers. As usual, too, they coveted Federal supplies. "Come on, boys, and charge!" yelled an encouraging sergeant, "they have cheese in their haversacks!" Yet the pride of the soldier stood higher than hunger. General D.H. Hill stooped to cheer a very badly wounded man. "What's your regiment?" asked Hill. "Fifth Confederate, New Orleans, and a damned good regiment it is," came the ready answer. - *Captains of the Civil War* by William Wood

STEUART'S BRIGADE RENEWING THE CONFEDERATE ATTACK ON CULP'S HILL, MORNING OF THE THIRD DAY.

Wounded Native Americans from the Battle of the Wilderness

Headquarters, Army of the Potomac, Brandy Station, Virginia; Company of Zouaves in foreground.

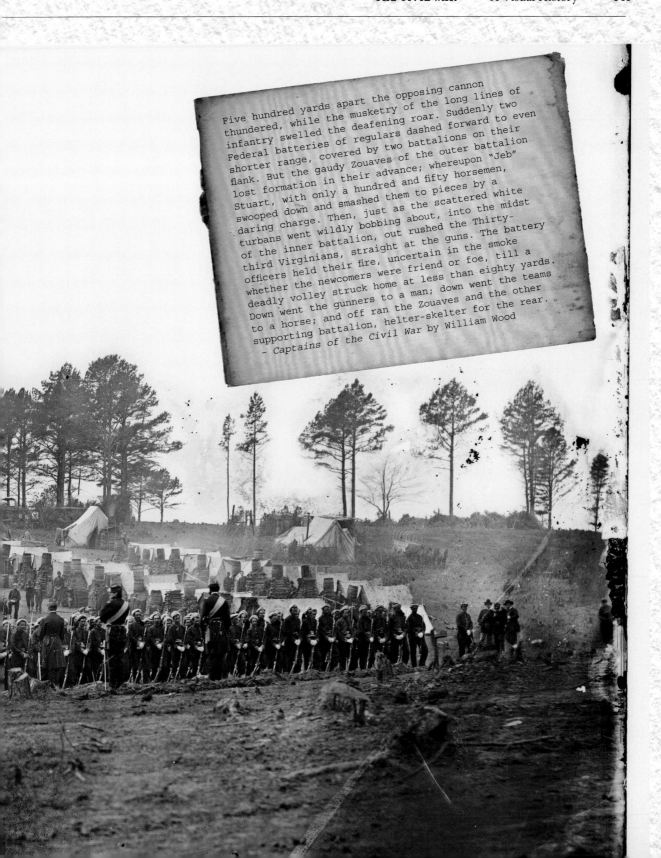

Five hundred yards apart the opposing cannon thundered, while the musketry of the long lines of infantry swelled the deafening roar. Suddenly two Federal batteries of regulars dashed forward to even shorter range, covered by two battalions on their flank. But the gaudy Zouaves of the outer battalion lost formation in their advance; whereupon "Jeb" Stuart, with only a hundred and fifty horsemen, swooped down and smashed them to pieces by a daring charge. Then, just as the scattered white turbans went wildly bobbing about, into the midst of the inner battalion, out rushed the Thirty-third Virginians, straight at the guns. The battery officers held their fire, uncertain in the smoke whether the newcomers were friend or foe, till a deadly volley struck home at less than eighty yards. Down went the gunners to a man; down went the teams to a horse; and off ran the Zouaves and the other supporting battalion, helter-skelter for the rear.
– Captains of the Civil War by William Wood

Cavalry in pursuit of infantry across farm near Falling Waters, Maryland

Dead horses on battlefield, Gettysburg, Pennsylvania

RICHMOND NEWSBOY ANNOUNCING THE REBEL SUCCESS!!!

ON THE WAY TO THE BATTLE OF GETTYSBURG
COMPANY L, SECOND "REGULARS"

The "Second" fought in the reserve brigade under General Merritt, during the second day of the battle. The leading figures in the picture are First-Sergeant Painter and First-Lieutenant Dewees. Few photographs show cavalry thus, in column.

Fall of General Lyon

Council of War General Ulysses S. Grant examining map held by General George G. Meade, Massaponax Church, Virginia

Dead Confederate sharpshooter at foot of Little Round Top, also known as Devil's Den, Pennsylvania

Siege of Vicksburg

HOME FRONT

I was truly glad to hear from home once more. I received the one from Rachel containing the photographs of the children which I prize very highly, nothing could have been sent me perhaps that I would have thought more of at this time, & little Carrie's too. I have thought so much about her, always, but that is all that is left of her for us here.

- Peter Wikoff, 86th Infantry, Illinois

Ma kiss our sweet little girl for me if she lives, and if she's dead have her buried nicely & plant two cedars or weeping willows at her grave one at head & feet. Carrie let me persuade you to be a brave little woman show yourself one of power one that can endure anything, this is all I have to write now in this short time, except it be to bid you goodbye while I remain your Devoted Husband.

~ Hiram Talbert Holt, 38th Infantry Alabama

FANNIE VIRGINIA CASSEOPIA LAWRENCE.
A Redeemed SLAVE CHILD, 5 years of age, as she ap-
peared when found in slavery. Redeemed in Virginia by Catharine
S. Lawrence. Baptized in Brooklyn at Plymouth Church, by
Henry Ward Beecher, May, 1863.

PHOTOGRAPHED BY
KELLOGG BROTHERS,
279 MAIN STREET,
HARTFORD, CONN.

Entered according to Act of Congress, in the year 1863, by C. S.
Lawrence, in the Clerk's Office of the District Court of the United
States, for the Southern District of New York.

TO COLORED MEN!

FREEDOM,

Protection, Pay, and a Call to Military Duty!

On the 1st day of January, 1863, the President of the United States proclaimed FREE-
DOM to over THREE MILLIONS OF SLAVES. This decree is to be enforced by all the power of
the Nation. On the 21st of July last he issued the following order:

PROTECTION OF COLORED TROOPS.

"WAR DEPARTMENT, ADJUTANT GENERAL'S OFFICE,
WASHINGTON, July 21.

"General Order, No. 233.

"The following order of the President is published for the information and government of all concerned:—

EXECUTIVE MANSION, WASHINGTON, July 30.

"It is the duty of every Government to give protection to its citizens, of whatever class, color, or condition, and especially to
those who are duly organized as soldiers in the public service. The law of nations, and the usages and customs of war, as carried on
by civilized powers, permit no distinction as to color in the treatment of prisoners of war as public enemies. To sell or enslave any
captured person on account of his color, is a relapse into barbarism, and a crime against the civilization of the age.

"The Government of the United States will give the same protection to all its soldiers, and if the enemy shall sell or enslave any
one because of his color, the offense shall be punished by retaliation upon the enemy's prisoners in our possession. It is, therefore,
ordered, for every soldier of the United States, killed in violation of the laws of war, a rebel soldier shall be executed; and for every
one enslaved by the enemy, or sold into slavery, a rebel soldier shall be placed at hard labor on the public works, and continued at such
labor until the other shall be released and receive the treatment due to prisoners of war.

"ABRAHAM LINCOLN."

"By order of the Secretary of War.

"E. D. TOWNSEND, Assistant Adjutant General."

That the President is in earnest the rebels soon began to find out, as witness the following order from his Secretary of War:

"WAR DEPARTMENT, WASHINGTON CITY, August 3, 1863.

"SIR: Your letter of the 3d inst., calling the attention of this Department to the cases of Orin H. Brown, William H. Johnston,
and Wm. Wilson, three colored men captured on the gunboat Isaac Smith, has received consideration. This Department has directed
that three rebel prisoners of South Carolina, if there be any such in our possession, and if not, three others, be confined in close custody
and held as hostages for Brown, Johnston and Wilson, and that the fact be communicated to the rebel authorities at Richmond.

"Very respectfully your obedient servant,

"EDWIN M. STANTON, Secretary of War.

"The Hon. GIDEON WELLES, Secretary of the Navy."

And retaliation will be our practice now—man for man—to the bitter end.

LETTER OF CHARLES SUMNER,

Written with reference to the Convention held at Poughkeepsie, July 15th and 16th, 1863, to promote Colored Enlistments.

BOSTON, July 13th, 1863.

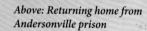

Above: Returning home from Andersonville prison

C. A. Haun parting from his Family before his Execution. (Page 313.)

C. Alexander Haun, a potter from Tennessee, was executed for conspiring to burn bridges controlled by Confederate forces

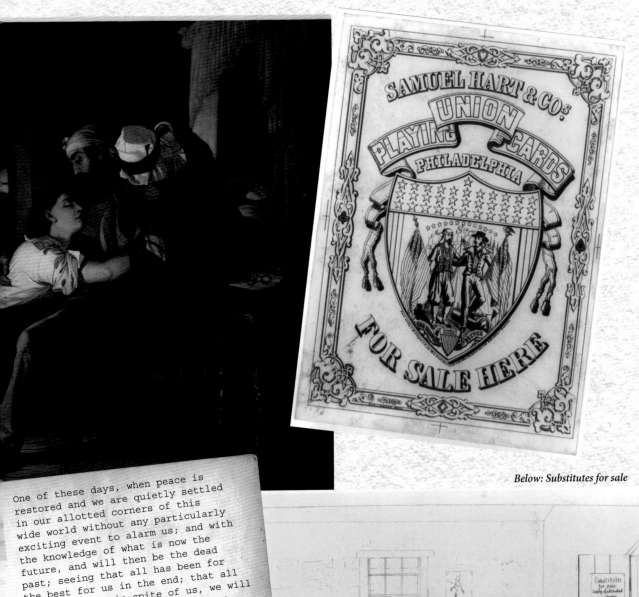

Below: Substitutes for sale

One of these days, when peace is restored and we are quietly settled in our allotted corners of this wide world without any particularly exciting event to alarm us; and with the knowledge of what is now the future, and will then be the dead past; seeing that all has been for the best for us in the end; that all has come right in spite of us, we will wonder how we could ever have been foolish enough to await each hour in such breathless anxiety. We will ask ourselves if it was really true that nightly, as we lay down to sleep, we did not dare plan for the morning, feeling that we might be homeless and beggars before the dawn. How unreal it will then seem! We will say it was our wild imagination, perhaps. But how bitterly, horribly true it is now! – A *Confederate Girl's Diary*, Sarah Morgan

Poor deluded Miss-Souri takes a Secession bath, and finds it much hotter than she expected!

GREAT EXCITEMENT IN South Carolina!

Was being caused before the war by the wonderful cures of Bronchitis, Asthma, Sore Throat, Consumption, &c., effected by Wishart's Pine Tree Tar Cordial, in and around Charleston.

BEAUREGARD

himself might as well be

A PRISONER!

as to be confined with a distressing Cough or Sore Throat and not be able to obtain Wishart's Pine Tree Tar Cordial, which is known to cure all Complaints of the Throat, Consumption, &c.

Depot, No. 10 North Second Street

Above: Notices and cartoons depicting the secession

Right: Former Vice President Breckinridge marked as a traitor by the Union for his allegiance to the C.S.A.

An Ordinance,

To dissolve the Union between the State of South Carolina and other States united with her under the compact entitled, "The Constitution of the United States of America."

We, the People of the State of South Carolina, in Convention assembled, do declare and ordain, and it is hereby declared and ordained,

That the Ordinance adopted by us in Convention, on the twenty-third day of May, in the year of our Lord one thousand seven hundred and eighty-eight, whereby the Constitution of the United States of America was ratified, and also, all Acts and parts of Acts of the General Assembly of this State, ratifying amendments of the said Constitution, are hereby repealed; and that the union now subsisting between South Carolina and other States, under the name of "The United States of America," is hereby dissolved.

Enlisting Irish and German immigrants at the Battery in New York City

Above: Captured flags

Left: Officers and ladies on porch of a garrison house, Fort Monroe, Virginia

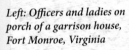

Right: John H. Morgan & wife, C.S.A.

HOME FRONT

Right: Mrs. General M. Vickers with long flowing hair, three-quarter length portrait, seated at table with open book

Above: *Cartoon printed in Harper's Bazaar in 1887.*
Mr. Stretcher: It was at Shiloh, Mrs. Keene, I had been hard hit, & was lying where I fell when ...
Mrs. Keene: Beg pardon, Mr. Stretcher, but how you must have changed your methods since then ...
Why now judging from the fact that Shiloh was fought 25 years ago, you must be lying where you stand.

Below: Maimed soldiers and others before office of the U.S. Christian Commission

Fashions for May–Spring Mantilla and child's dress

Francis Preston Blair and his wife, Violet Gist, as they looked at the end of the Civil War

Departure for the War

Returning home

Family of slaves at the Gaines' house

The burning of an orphan asylum during the draft riots of 1863 in New York City

HOME FRONT

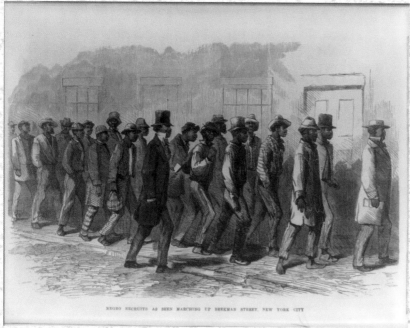

Union prisoners in a Rebel town

Top: Union recruits
Bottom: Woman wearing mourning brooch and displaying framed image of soldier

A mother holding hand of her son, a Union soldier

The soldier going off to war

FRANK LESLIE'S ILLUSTRATED NEWSPAPER.   [MAY 10, 1862.

BEAUREGARD ACCEPTS THE ALTERNATIVE.
General Beauregard declared in his address to the Rebel soldiers on the morning of the Battle of Pittsburg Landing: *" I will water
my horse in the Tennessee River or in h—ll before night."*

*General Beauregard being
tormented by demons, as his
horse drinks from burning
water, in hell*

THE SOLDIER'S DREAM OF HOME.

The soldier's dream of home

Left: Unidentified soldier in Union uniform holding a young child in his lap.

Southern women feeling the effects of the rebellion, and creating bread riots

Union refugees

HOME FRONT

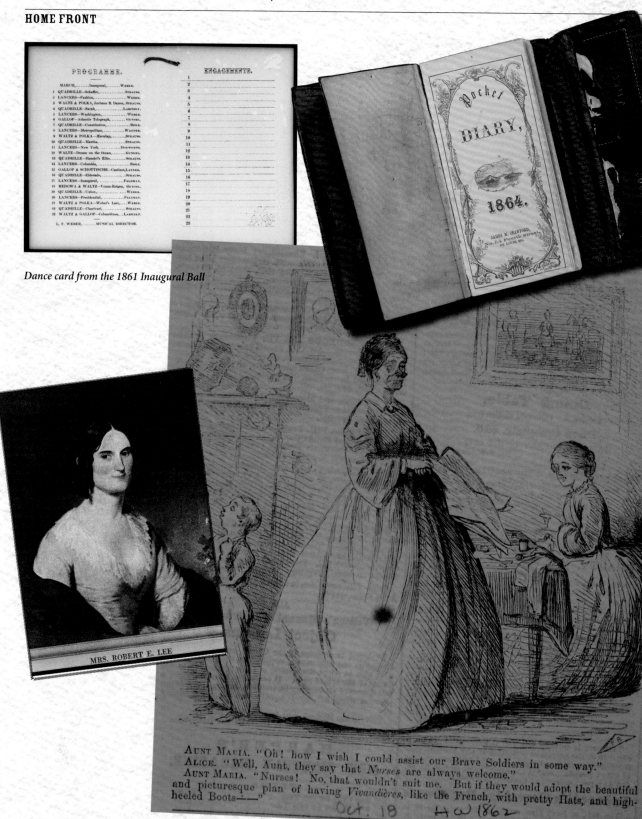

Dance card from the 1861 Inaugural Ball

MRS. ROBERT E. LEE

AUNT MARIA. "Oh! how I wish I could assist our Brave Soldiers in some way."
ALICE. "Well, Aunt, they say that *Nurses* are always welcome."
AUNT MARIA. "Nurses! No, that wouldn't suit me. But if they would adopt the beautiful and picturesque plan of having *Vivandières*, like the French, with pretty Hats, and high-heeled Boots——"

John L. Burns, the "old hero of Gettysburg"

Off for the War

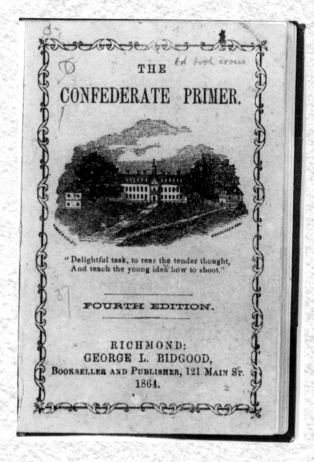

Opposite page, top: Cartoon contrasting the "Misery and bondage" of the South with the "Happiness and civilization" of the North

Left: JIsaac and Rosa, slave children from New Orleans

A GOOD WAY FOR FATHERS OF FAMILIES TO AID RECRUITING.

PRISONS

He was taken to Cahaba prison, Alabama, and there his treatment was horrible. He was captured in September, 1864, and in March 1865, the river overflowed, the prison was flooded, and the prisoners were obliged to stand in water up to their waists for one week. He weighed 130 pounds when he entered, and on coming out, in March, weighed by sixty pounds.

–Biographical Sketch of C.A. Sloane, 2nd Ohio Infantry

But here's the ration: The strong sustained life on four ounces of sour light bread and three ounces of salt beef or pork for breakfast; for dinner, the same amount of bread was allowed, and, in lieu of the meat, a compound called soup, but in reality nothing more than hot salty water, in which bags of peas or beans had been boiled, but which were carefully removed and kept for other uses than to make animal heat for cold, starving prisoners of war.

-G. W. D. Porter, 44th Tennessee Regiment.

UNION SOLDIERS IN ANDERSONVILLE PRISON.
SICKNESS,—STARVATION,—DEATH.

AND THEN ON THIS!

SOLDIERS! HAVE YOU FOUGHT IN VAIN?

THE CONTRAST OF SUFFERING ANDERSONVILLE & FORTRESS MONROE

SOLDIERS! LOOK ON THIS PICTURE.

SHALL THE REBEL LEADERS BE RESTORED TO POWER?

TREASON MUST BE MADE ODIOUS. ANDREW JOHNSON.

THE REBEL LEADER, JEFF DAVIS, AT FORTRESS MONROE.
HEALTH,—PLENTY,—LUXURY.

PRISONS

Libby Prison

The building is of brick, with a front of near one hundred and forty feet, and one hundred feet deep. It is divided into nine rooms; the ceilings are low, and ventilation imperfect; the windows are barred, through which the windings of James River and the tents of Belle Isle may be seen. Its immediate surroundings are far from being agreeable; the sentinels pacing the streets constantly are unpleasant reminders that your stay is not a matter of choice; and were it so, few would choose it long as a boarding-house. In this building were crowded about one thousand officers of nearly every grade, not one of whom was permitted to go out till exchanged or released by death.
– *Four Months in Libby* by Isaac N. Johnston

To men accustomed to an active life this mode of existence soon became exceedingly irksome, and innumerable methods were soon devised to make the hours pass less wearily. A penknife was made to do the duty of a complete set of tools, and it was marvelous to see the wonders achieved by that single instrument. – *Four Months in Libby* by Isaac N. Johnston

Provost Marshal—and police of Alexandria searching and examining a prisoner of war

Now on Exhibition, the Celebrated BLOOD HOUNDS

HERO and SPOT.

The MONSTER BLOOD HOUND HERO! from Castle Thunder and Libby Prison, Richmond, Va., the Largest Dog in the World, weighing 208 Pounds. He is 7 feet, 3½ inches from tip to tip, stands 5 feet 6 inches high, and measures 18 in. across the breast.

HERO is accompanied by the Celebrated CUBAN BLOOD HOUND SPOT, from the ANDERSONVILLE PRISON.

☞ **Don't Fail to See Them!** ◄

PRISONS

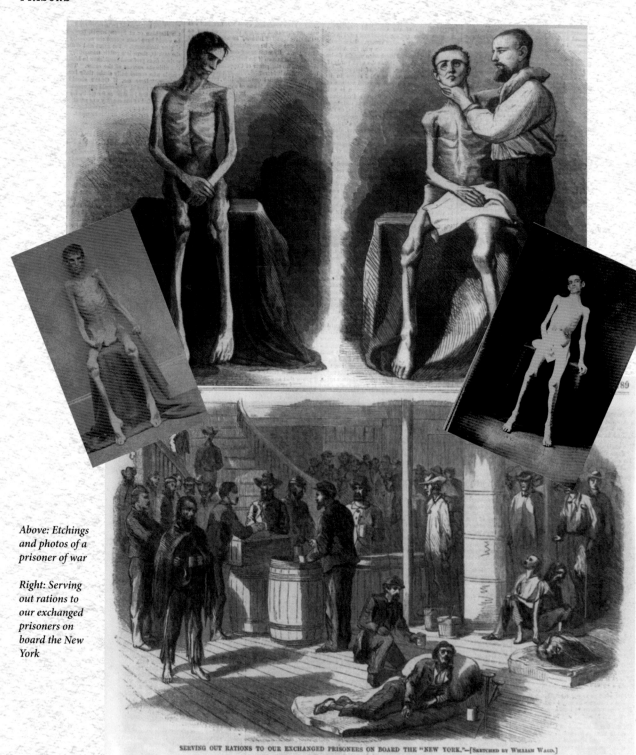

Above: Etchings and photos of a prisoner of war

Right: Serving out rations to our exchanged prisoners on board the New York

SERVING OUT RATIONS TO OUR EXCHANGED PRISONERS ON BOARD THE "NEW YORK."—[SKETCHED BY WILLIAM WAUD.]

OUR EXCHANGED PRISONERS

No more touching scene has occurred during the war than that which glorified the deck of the *Eliza Hancox*, Colonel MULFORD's dispatch boat, on Friday November 19, which .....

by want and home-sickness have been brought to the verge of idiocy, or been smitten for months with almost hopeless melancholy, shout for the old flag and for Colonel MULFORD, and, regardless of the presence of their rebel companions, sing, ...

of SHERMAN's march. We hope that SHERMAN will compensate for this by redeeming all our prisoners at Milen. The prison-camp at Andersonville was almost entirely vacated early in November; east of Milledgeville a few miles is "Camp .....

extravagant malice—when even the rebel surgeons protested and entered complaints which more than bear out the statements which we have received from returned prisoners—then the prison was broken up and the prisoners dispersed. The regulations .....

Andersonville Prison

May 12 — Raining hard all day, and fighting all last night. About 2 o'clock this afternoon about 2,000 prisoners came in, with them Major-General Johnson and Brigadier-General Stewart. We have moved four miles nearer to Fredericksburg. I suppose they think we are too close to our own lines, and they are afraid we will be recaptured, as it was a few days ago. We heard our boys', or, as the Yankees call it, the Rebel yell. We prisoners also gave the Rebel yell. A few minutes after that they brought cannon to bear on us, and we were told to stop, or they would open on us. We stopped. - Louis Leon, 1st Infantry, North Carolina

Confederate prisoners at Belle Plain Landing, Virginia, captured with Johnson's Division, May 12, 1864

PRISONS

It was well you left Petersburg when you did, for the very next day our extreme right was attacked, and, as our line was very thin, it was easily broken. Billie was digging a rifle pit when some Yankees charged it and captured all who were at work on it, and he is now a prisoner.

During the day a few prisoners were brought back, and among them was a smoke-begrimed captain with gray hair. I invited him into my tent and gave him something 'to eat. He had been in some of the hardest fighting of the war, and he said to me: "You see these white hairs. When I came into the army they were all coal black."

As night came on many wounded were brought back to some huts lately occupied by soldiers, but now used by us as a hospital. Among them was Mose Cappocks, and I amputated his thumb. General Hill was killed.

The next day we began to leave, and there was continuous fighting. Our march soon developed into a disastrous retreat, and we were pushed to the extreme every hour of it for eight days. At Sailors Creek we were compelled to abandon our wagons, and they were burned. In one of them I had a new case of the finest surgical instruments. They had recently run the blockade and I hated to see them destroyed.

General Kershaw and his young son were captured here. I saw some Yankee spies in gray uniforms marched along with us under guard. They had been captured in our lines, but the surrender occurring so soon afterwards saved them from being hung.

Spencer Glasglow Welch, 13th Infantry South Carolina, May 1865

Above: General Hill

Bottom left: Rampart where Hill served

Bottom right: Union prisoner's occupation

Slave pen, interior view, Alexandria, Virginia

Hut which was used as a hospital

Front of "slave pen," Alexandria, Virginia

PRISONS

Andersonville Prison

Confederate prisoners at railroad depot, Chattanooga, Tennessee

Belle Boyd, Confederate spy

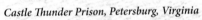

Castle Thunder Prison, Petersburg, Virginia

PRISONS

We began fixing up what little we could to protect ourselves against the weather. Cold as this was we decided that it was safer to endure it and risk frost-biting every night than to build one of the mud-walled and mud-covered holes that so many lived in. These were much warmer than lying out on the frozen ground, but we believed that they were very unhealthy, and that no one lived long who inhabited them.
So we set about repairing our faithful old blanket—now full of great holes. We watched the dead men to get pieces of cloth from their garments to make patches, which we sewed on with yarn raveled from other fragments of woolen cloth. Some of our company, whom we found in the prison, donated us the three sticks necessary to make tent-poles—wonderful generosity when the preciousness of firewood is remembered. We hoisted our blanket upon these; built a wall of mud bricks at one end, and in it a little fireplace to economize our scanty fuel to the last degree, and were once more at home, and much better off than most of our neighbors.
The pinching cold cured me of my repugnance to wearing dead men's clothes, or rather it made my nakedness so painful that I was glad to cover it as best I could, and I began foraging among the corpses for garments. I found that dying men with good clothes were as carefully watched over by sets of fellows who constituted themselves their residuary legatees as if they were men of fortune dying in the midst of a circle of expectant nephews and nieces. Before one was fairly cold his clothes would be appropriated and divided, and I have seen many sharp fights between contesting claimants.
– John McElroy, Andersonville

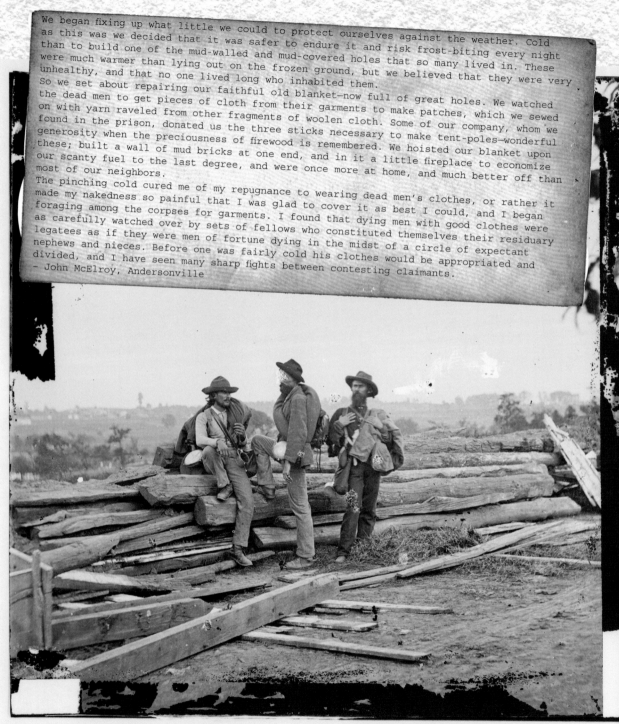

Above: Three Confederate prisoners, Gettysburg, Pennsylvania

Right: Mrs. Greenhow, Confederate spy, and daughter (imprisoned in old Capitol Prison in Washington, D.C.)

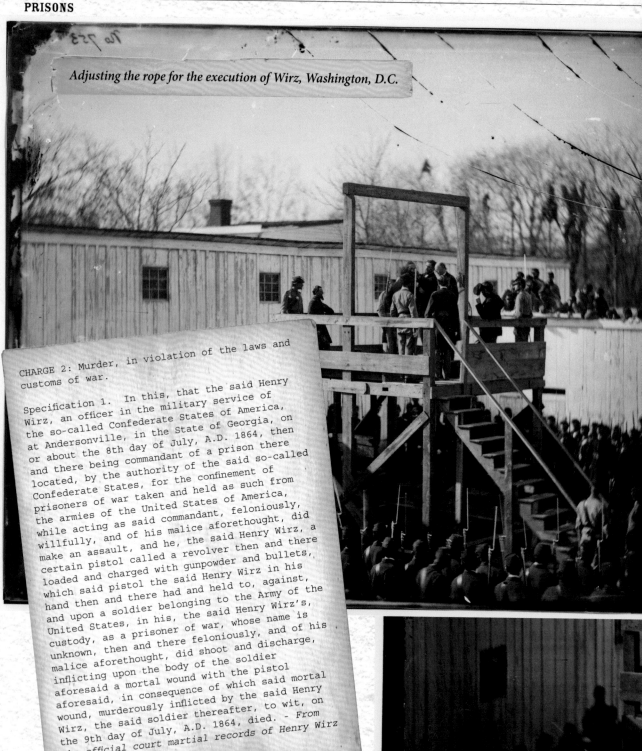

Adjusting the rope for the execution of Wirz, Washington, D.C.

CHARGE 2: Murder, in violation of the laws and customs of war.

Specification 1. In this, that the said Henry Wirz, an officer in the military service of the so-called Confederate States of America, at Andersonville, in the State of Georgia, on or about the 8th day of July, A.D. 1864, then and there being commandant of a prison there located, by the authority of the said so-called Confederate States, for the confinement of prisoners of war taken and held as such from the armies of the United States of America, while acting as said commandant, feloniously, willfully, and of his malice aforethought, did make an assault, and he, the said Henry Wirz, a certain pistol called a revolver then and there loaded and charged with gunpowder and bullets, which said pistol the said Henry Wirz in his hand then and there had and held to, against, and upon a soldier belonging to the Army of the United States, in his, the said Henry Wirz's, custody, as a prisoner of war, whose name is unknown, then and there feloniously, and of his malice aforethought, did shoot and discharge, inflicting upon the body of the soldier aforesaid a mortal wound with the pistol aforesaid, in consequence of which said mortal wound, murderously inflicted by the said Henry Wirz, the said soldier thereafter, to wit, on the 9th day of July, A.D. 1864, died. - From the official court martial records of Henry Wirz

Hooded body of Captain Wirz hanging from the scaffold with some spectators watching from nearby trees, Washington, D.C.

BATTLES

†

FALL OF THE CONFEDERACY

★ ★ ★ ★ ★ ★ ★ ★ ★ ★

Grant met Lee at McLean's private residence near Appomattox Court House. There was a remarkable contrast between the appearances of the two commanders. Grant, only forty-three, and without a tinge of gray in his brown hair, took an inch or two off his medium height by stooping keenly forward, and had nothing in his shabby private's uniform to show his rank except the three-starred shoulder-straps. When the main business was over, and he had time to notice details, he apologized to Lee, explaining that the extreme rapidity of his movements had carried him far ahead of his baggage.

Captains of the War *by William Wood*

The Confederates had been obliged to reduce themselves simply to what they stood in, each officer had naturally put on his best. Hence Lee's magnificent appearance in a brand-new general's uniform with the jeweled sword of honor that Virginia had given him. Well over six feet tall, straight as an arrow in spite of his fifty-eight years and snow-white, war-grown beard, still extremely handsome, and full of equal dignity and charm, he looked, from head to foot, the perfect leader of devoted men

Captains of the War *by William Wood..*

The surrender of General Lee

Ruins of paper mill near Richmond

This is a piece of the
rebel flag taken from Corinth
by the first man that
entered the breastworks
(Genuine)
the "Union Club" Feby 22 1864

Grant and his generals on horseback

*Confederate returns
to a burned home and
murdered wife*

*Wagon train of Military
Telegraph Corps*

BATTLES † **FALL OF THE CONFEDERACY**

Capture of Savannah

REBEL PRISONERS, UNDER ORDERS OF GEN. SHERMAN, TAKING UP THE TORPEDOES IN FRONT OF FORT M'ALLISTER, CAPTURED BY THE UNION FORCES, DEC. 15.—FROM A SKETCH BY OUR SPECIAL ARTIST, W. T. CRANE.

CAPTURE OF SAVANNAH—GEN. GEARY ISSUING PASSES TO CITIZENS.

REAR OF THUNDERBOLT

Thunderbolt Battery

View of Fort McAllister

Bombardment of Fort Fisher

13-inch mortar cannon called "The Dictator"

BATTLES   †   FALL OF THE CONFEDERACY

Antietam

Cedar Mountain

Railroad gun

CAPITULATION & SURRENDER OF ROBT E LEE & HIS ARMY AT APPOMATTOX CH.VA TO LT GENL U.S.GRANT.
APRIL 9TH 1865.

Above: General Sherman's advance, Buzzard's Roost Pass, Georgia

Left: Confederate soldiers as they fell inside the fence on the Hagerstown road

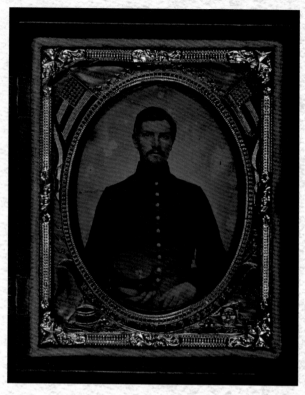

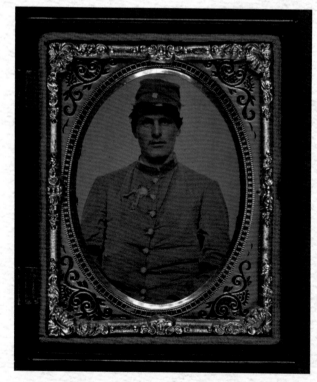

Soldier's portraits from Liljenquist Collection

GENERAL SHERMAN'S ADVANCE—BUZZARD'S ROOST PASS, GEORGIA.—[See Page 191.]

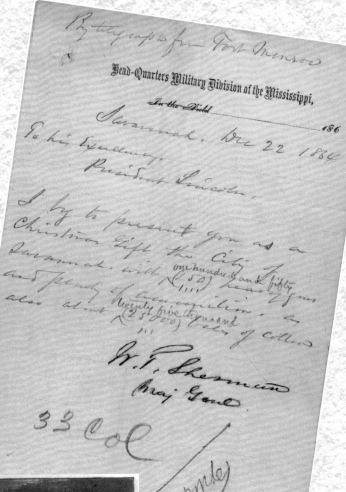

Letter from Sherman "giving" Lincoln the surrender of Savannah

GENERAL SHERMAN'S ADVANCE—VIEW OF KENESAW MOUNTAIN, FROM LITTLE KENESAW.—[Sketched by T. R. Davis.]

THE AFTERMATH

I suppose you have heard ere this of the death of your son Robert, who was wounded on the 15th of Dec, while gallantly advancing in a charge on the enemies' works. Robert was a good brave soldier, and his death is deeply felt by all his comrades, and none more than myself. I tender you my heartfelt sympathies, and assure you that while you lose a beloved son, I lose an esteemed friend and fellow soldier.

– Thomas Turner, 1st Sargeant., Co. H

How often have I said during the war that I would thank my God if I could once more be at home with my little family and a piece of bread. If I had anything more I would highly appreciate it, but if not I could be happy. I returned home to my family. I had the bread; I also had plenty of other things, or at least as much as nature called for. I was once more a free and happy man.

– J. W. Reid

Soldiers' Cemetery, Alexandria, Virginia

THE AFTERMATH

As darkness came upon the city confusion and disorder increased. People were running about everywhere with plunder and provisions. Barrels and boxes were rolled and tumbled about the streets as they had been all day. Barrels of liquor were broken open and the gutters ran with whiskey and molasses.

In the pale dawn I saw a light shoot up from Shockoe Warehouse. Presently soldiers came running down the streets. Some carried balls of tar; some carried torches. As they ran they fired the balls of tar and pitched them onto the roofs of prominent houses and into the windows of public buildings and churches. I saw balls pitched on the roof of General R. E. Lee's home. As the day grew lighter I saw a Confederate soldier on horseback pause almost under my window. He wheeled and fired behind him; rode a short distance, wheeled and fired again; and so on, wheeling and firing as he went until he was out of sight. Coming up the street from that end toward which his fire had been directed and from which he had come, rode a body of men in blue uniforms. It was not a very large body, they rode slowly, and passed just beneath my window. Exactly at eight o'clock the Confederate flag that fluttered above the Capitol came down and the Stars and Stripes were run up. We knew what that meant! The song "On to Richmond!" was ended. Richmond was in the hands of the Federals. We covered our faces and cried aloud. All through the house was the sound of sobbing. It was as the house of mourning, the house of death. - A *Virginia Girl in the Civil War* by Myrta Lockett Avary,

Above: The ruins of Richmond
Below: The ruins of Charleston

Above: Cover of the New York Times *declaring the end of the war*

Top left: Cartoon depicting Jeff Davis disguised as a woman during his attempted escape

Bottom left: Cartoon contrasting presidential candidates Andrew Jackson and George McClellan

THE AFTERMATH

Above and right: Lewis Payne, Booth associate who attempted to assassinate Secretary of State William Seward

Rope used to hang the Lincoln conspirators

Flags at half mast and mourning banners displayed at the Capitol

Below: Scene of Lincoln's death

THE AFTERMATH

Left: Graves of sailors killed during the bombardment of November 7, 1861, Hilton Head, South Carolina

Right: Men repairing single-track railroad after Battle of Stone's River, Tennessee

Boxcars with refugees at Atlanta railroad depot

2663

THE AFTERMATH

PROCLAMATION OF EMANCIPATION.

Left: Family arriving at Union lines

THE LOST CAUSE.

General Edward O.C. Ord, wife and child at the residence of Jefferson Davis. In the doorway is the table on which the surrender of General Robert E. Lee was signed.

The last offer of reconciliation in remembrance of President Lincoln.

Co. in the Clerk's Office of the District Court of the U.S. for the So. District of New-York.

Preparing to raise the old flag at Fort Sumter

THE AFTERMATH

Sherman's men destroying railroad, Atlanta, Georgia

The capture of Jefferson Davis

THE
OST CAUSE

LEE.   DAVIS.   JACKSON.

DEO VINDICE

nothing on God's earth now;
the waters below it ;
of a nation that passed away,
l, and show it.
who will lend an ear
rifle will tell,
a patriot's dream,
ation that fell.

ss the precious ores,
f a stranger to borrow;
y our "promise to pay,"
redeem on the morrow.
ed on, and weeks became years,
rs were empty still;
o scarce, the Treasury quaked
r should drop in the till,

But the faith that was in us was strong indeed,
Though our poverty well we discerned,
And this little note represented the pay
That our suffering veterans earned.
They knew it had hardly a value in gold,
But as gold our soldiers received it ;
It gazed in our eyes with a promise to pay,
And every true soldier believed it.

But our boys thought little of price or pay,
Or of bills that were overdue,
We knew if it bought our bread to-day,
T'was the best our poor Country could do.
Keep it, it tells all our history o'er,
From the birth of the dream to its last ;
Modest, and born of the Angel Hope
Like our hope of success, It Passed.

FORT SUMTER 1861   JOHNSON.   BEAUREGARD   APPOMATTOX C.H. 1865

THE AFTERMATH

Composite of scenes at the end of the Civil War, including homeward march

"Radical" members of the first legislature after the war, South Carolina

THE AFTERMATH

HARPER'S WEEKLY

HOME FROM THE WAR.

Homecoming

Facing page: General Lee at the table where he signed the surrender

Editor's Notes

Our culture has become accustomed to rapid communication and instantaneous photographs which make it difficult to appreciate the challenges of writing a letter or taking a photograph from the front lines of the Civil War. In the midst of a campaign or while on the march, having the time to write a letter was a luxury. Smoke from the guns and cannons often obscured the view of the camera lenses during battles, and the rapid movement of the troops made taking photos during decisive moments on the battlefield nearly impossible. Cameras had to be in focus before the glass plate was prepared to capture a photo, so scenes from the front lines were best taken from a distance or left to artists to portray. Sketches and engravings were eagerly anticipated by those at home, as were the photographs revealing the war efforts behind the scenes and within the camps. Daguerreotype portraits became popular at this time as family members longed for keepsake photographs of their loved ones should they become casualties of the war.

In this history we have included letters, speeches and memoirs to capture the emotions and thoughts of those who were witnessing these events. When possible we have featured photographs or illustrations of these same moments being described. Together, they give us a more thorough understanding of this war which cost over 600,000 lives.

Special Thanks

This collection of images contains rarely seen photos, lithographs and posters from the Great War between the States. These images were brought to life on these pages by the careful and beautiful design of Pilar Taylor. Without the kind assistance of the staff at the Library of Congress and the National Archives, this book would not have been possible. Our special thanks to these keepers of our collective national memory and treasures: Barbara Natanson, Marilyn Ibach, Jeff Bridgers and Jewel McPherson. Additional thanks to our intrepid researchers: Michele Gay, Lynda Cardwell, Dagny Leonard and Katherine Quinn. Few photographs survived the burning of the cities throughout the South, and we were grateful to Ann Drury Wellford and Robert Hancock at the Museum of the Confederacy for their help in procuring those rare images. Finally, we wish to thank the Liljenquist family for their donation to the Library of Congress of more than 700 ambrotype and tintype photographs of soldiers from both sides of the war, some of which are included in this book.

CREDITS

All images, unless otherwise noted, are courtesy of the Library of Congress. **5** Inauguration of President Abraham Lincoln, LC-USZ62-12950 **6** Inspection and sale of a slave, LC-USZ62-39380; Slave Pen, Alexandria, VA, LC-USZ62-65306 ; $100 Reward!, LC-USZ62-39380 **7** Lincoln campaign button, LC-USZ62-126415; House that Jeff built, LC-USZ62-12963; Governor Robert Hayne, Inaugural speech, December 13, 1830 **8** Secession Hall, LC-DIG-ppmsca-19336 **9** Frank Leslie's illustrated newspaper, LC-USZ62-109704; The inauguration of Jefferson Davis, LC-USZC4-1498; Jefferson Davis, LOC, LOT 13301, no. 1 **10** The Pending Conflict, LC-USZ62-42025; The Union Dissolved, LC-USZ62-11191; The first flag of independence raised in the South, LC-USZC4-4584 **11** Letter that accompanied The Great Seal of the Confederacy to the Library of Congress, PGA - Graham; Treasury Seal, LC-USZ62-51119; Confederate money, LOC, Lot 4421 **12** The unveiling of the Confederate flag, LC-USZ62-50858; The Great Seal of the Confederacy to the Library of Congress, PGA – Graham **13** The Great Seal of the Confederacy to the Library of Congress, PGA - Graham **15** Fort Sumter, LC-USZ62-15620 **16** Fort Sumter, LOC, DRWG/US - Key, no. 1 **17** The demand for the surrender of New Orleans, LC-USZ62-85797; Attack on the Massachusetts 6th at Baltimore, April 19, 1861, LC-USZ62-56105 **18**; Massachusetts Militia fighting with Confederate sympathizers in Baltimore, LC-USZ62-45871 **19** The last charge at the Battle of Shiloh, LC-USZ62-48871 **20** Battle of Shiloh, LC-USZ62-48871 **22** Bull Run, VA, Sudley church through the trees, LC-DIG-cwpb-01300 **24** Breaching battery against Fort Sumter, LC-DIG-cwpb-04734; Interior of Fort Sumter, LC-USZC2-2663 **26** Mock battery, LC-DIG-cwpb-00749 **27** Port Royal evacuation, LC-DIG-cwpb-01812 **28** Cedar Mountain, VA. Federal battery fording a tributary of the Rappahannock on the day of battle, LC-DIG-cwpb-00220 **30** Fifteen inch gun used in the defense of Washington, DC, LC-USZ62-84372 **32** Sullivan's Island, S.C, . Exploded gun in Confederate battery, LC-DIG-cwpb-00176; Views of Confederate fort near Atlanta, LOC, PH Baynard, No. 75; Confederate fortifications with Quaker guns, LOT 4166K **33** Confederate lines west of Atlanta, LOC, PH Baynard, No. 75; The "Marsh Battery", LC-DIG-cwpb-04737 **34** Captain Perkin's "Secesh" horse, LC-DIG-cwpb-0162; Confederate fortifications near Atlanta, LOC, PH Baynard, No. 75 **35** Charleston, S.C. Interior view of Castle Pinckney, LC-DIG-cwpb-02454; **35** Bombproof for telegraph operator on Morris Island, SC, LOC, PH Baynard, No. 75 **36** Lee's men, LC-USZ62-87170 **37** Cooks in the kitchen of Soldiers' Rest, LC-DIG-cwpb-04280; Snowball battle near Dalton, GA, LC-DIG-ppmsca-21383 **38** Nick Biddle, the first man wounded in the War Between the States, LC-USZ62-126417; Horse artillery on parade grounds, LC-USZC4-7980 **39** Unidentified young soldier in Confederate shell jacket and forage cap with single shot pistol, LC-DIG-ppmsca-27171 **40** Sherman, leaning on breach of gun, outside Atlanta, LC-DIG-cwpb-03384 **42** The "Wizard", LOC, Lot 13958 **44** Parrot rifle after bursting of muzzle, LC-DIG-cwpb-04726 **46** Display of Field Artillery, LOC, Lot 13958 **47** Professor Lowe's balloon EAGLE in a storm, LC-USZ62-42856; Confederate naval battery at Yorktown, VA; LC-USZ62-49299 **48** Bringing Parrott gun into position, LC-DIG-ppmsca-11714; Sling for transporting big guns, LC-DIG-cwpb-01361 **49** Removing munitions from captured fort, LC-B811- 3503, LOT 4166-G; Artillery battalion, LOC, Lot 13958 **50** City Point, VA, LC-DIG-cwpb-03926 **52** Grounded Confederate torpedo boat in Charleston, SC, National Archives; Captain Joseph Banks Lyle, C.S.A, National Archives **53** Major General Prince Polignac, National Archives; Camp of Confederate soldiers, National Archives **54** The Robert E. Lee I and The Great Republic, LOC, LOT 2939; Confederate soldiers, LOC, LOT 4421; EAM Sloop of War, LOC, LOT 12020 **56** The transport Black awk, LC-USZ62-61842 **57** Professor Lowe's military balloon near Gaines Mill, VA, LC-USZC4-7995; Gunboat Commodore McDonough, LC-USZ62-49371 **58** Integrated Union Naval crew, National Archives **59** The RATTLER - leader of the "Land Cruise" in 1863, LC-USZ62-61840; A besieging "tinclad" - the Marmora LC-USZ62-61841 **60** Butler's dredge-boat, sunk by a Confederate shell, LC-B811- 2550 **62** Muskets used as a coatrack, LC-USZ62-46137; Confederate Cartoon, LC-USZ62-33845; Confederate playing card, LOC, PR 13 CN 1968:168; Camp Cameron, LC-USZ62-126533 **63** Lieutenants George A. Custer, Nicolas Bowen, and William G. Jones, LC-DIG-cwpb-01007; Cockfighting at General Wilcox's headquarters, LC-DIG-cwpb-03895 **64** Bomb-proof quarters, LC-DIG-cwpb-01926; Federal encampment on Pamunkey River, VA, LC-DIG-cwpb-01402 **65** General William F. Bartlett and staff, LOC, LOT 4421; On guard, father and son, LC-USZ62-100755 **66** Provost Marshal Department, LC-DIG-cwpb-04032 **67** On skirmish line, LOC, DRWG/US - Waud, no. 146; African Americans on horseback leaving fields, LOC, DRWG/US - Waud, no. 54; Carrying the powder, LOC, DRWG/US - Waud, no. 52 **68** Dead Confederate soldier, LC-B811- 3175 **69** View of Knoxville from Fort Stanley, LOC, PH - Barnard, G.; View of Atlanta, LOC, PH - Barnard, G. **71** Lieutenants, LC-B811- 435A **72** Greenwall, LOC, LOT 13301, no. 164; Cook stove on U.S.S. MomitorR, LC-B815- 660 **73** Micah Jenkins, Brigadier General, C.S.A, National Archives; General A.J. Vaughn, of Texas, C.S.A, National Archives; Photograph of Confederate artillery loading, near Charleston, SC, National Archives **74** New Hampshire 3rd Infantry, Company A, LOC, LOT 10385 **75** Official stationery of Brig. General Frederick West Lander, LC-USZ62-63381; Map of the Battle of Wilson's Creek, Illus. in E468.A135 **76** Bodies of Confederate dead gathered for burial, LC-B811- 557 **77** Lincoln's Gettysburg Address, LC-B8184- 10454 **79** Bombardment and Capture of Fredericksburg, LOC **80** Savage Station, LC-USZ62-47275; Battlefield of Bull Run, LC-USZ62-62595; The battle of Pittsburgh, TN, LOC, Illus. in AP2.L52 1862; The late Rebel raid at Garlick Station, LC-USZ62-47635; Battle of Savage's Station, LC-USZ61-520 **81** Lee to the Rear, LOC, LOT 4416-K; Running ammunition trains into the Chickahominy, LC-USZ61-519 **79** Sentry in Chattanooga, TN, LOC, LOT 12020 **84** View on Battlefield of Antietam, LC-B815- 569 **86** Drilling troops near Washington, DC, LOC, LOT 4173 **87** Sic semper tyrannis - 22th Regt. U.S. Colored Troops, LOC, LOT 6592, no. 132 **88** Confederate Chieftans, LC-USZ62-111515 **89** Edward Ferrero, Colonel, Maj. General John Alexander Logan, LC-B817- 7053, LOT 4186-F; Benjamin Franklin Fisher, LC-USZ62-62943; Captain George Stoneman, LC-B811- 436, LOT 4186-S **90** Capture of Fort Donelson, TN, LOC, LOT 4416 F; Charge of General Smith's division, LOC, LOT 4417 **91** Tripod signal, LC-B811- 3661; General Osterhaus, LC-USZ62-31497 **92** The demand for the surrender of New Orleans, LOC, LOT 4416; Scouts and guides for the Army of the Potomac, LC-B817- 7294; General Lee on horseback, LOC, LOT 4421 B **94** Naval Attack at Forts Jackson, LOC, LOT 4209; Battle of Lexington, MS, LC-USZ62-42580; Fed observation balloon being inflated, LOT 4172-A **95** Camp of 3rd New Hampshire Infantry, LOC, LOT 10385; NH Infantry, LOC, LOT 10385 **96** Long Bridge over the Potomac, National Archives **97** Confederate flag, PGA - McRae, J.C **98** Famous Union Commanders, LC-DIG-pga-02749 **100** Our Heroes, LC-DIG-pga-03338 **101** Cooper Shop Refreshment Saloon, LC-DIG-pga-02892 **102** Rev. Dr. Clifford H. Plumer, Clergy, LOT 6592, no. 60; W.B. Hatch, Col. 4th NJ Infantry, LOT 4192; J. Albert Monroe, Lt. Col, LOT 7881; Ulysses S. Grant, LC-USZ62-95560 **103** Grant from West Point to Appomattox, LC-DIG-pga-02394 **104** Band of 107th U.S. Colored Infantry, LOT 4190-E; Roll of Honor, LC-USZC4-5152; Sharp Shooters, LC-USZ62-32375 **105** Elmira Coronet Band, LOT 4190-E **107** Confederate hospital near Richmond, VA, LOC, LOT 11486-E, no. 13 **108** Camp of 31st Pennsylvania Infantry, LOT 4190-E; Vivandiere, LOC, PH - Fenton (R.), no. 103 **109** Tending a horse, LOC, LOT 14022, no. 7; Soldiers at table eating, LOC, LOT 10385; Walt Whitman, National Archives **111** Captain Sellers and wife at Fort Totten, LC-B817- 7658; Brother Jonathan, LOC, Illus. in AP101.Y35 **112** Two women trimming a soldier's hair, LOC, DRWG/US - Waud, no. 221 **113** Government repair shops, LC-B817- 7880; Marriage in a camp, LOC, DRWG/US - Waud, no. 196 **115** Scouts and guides, Army of the Potomac, LC-B817- 7294; Burial of soldier, LC-B811- 721 **117** Union blacksmith shop, LC-B817- 7699 **119** Constructing road on south bank of North Anna River, LC-B817- 7304; Fort Fisher, NC,

CREDITS

LC-B817- 7195; Mathew Brady's photography outfit in the field, LOC, LOT 4172 **121** 1st Virginia Cavalry at a halt, LOC, DRWG/US - Waud, no. 764; Alfred Waud, LC-B815- 254 **122** James Walker and Theodore Davis, LOC, LOT 6592, no. 161; Theodore Russell Davis, LOC, LOT 9628; General Ambrose E. Burnside with Mathew B. Brady, LC-B811- 2433; Photographer Timothy O'Sullivan at Manassas, LOC, LOT 4167 **124** Bridge at Strawberry Plains, LC-B811- 2665 **125** Engine Commodore, LOC, LOT 11486-C, no. 17; Picnic party at Antietam bridge, LC-B815- 581 **126** Rebecca Pomroy, LOC, LOT 6286; Columbia College Hospital, LC-B817- 7924 **127** Portion of a speech by Clara Barton, LOC, Item in MSS Coll. c-Mss Div **128** Embalming surgeon at work on soldier's body, LC-B811- 2531 **129** Straw huts erected on Smith's, LC-B815- 592 **131** Amputation being performed in a mobile hospital, National Archives; Orphaned boys of Civil War soldiers, LOC, LOT 6341; Civil War surgeon Mary E. Walker, LOC, LOT 12661, no. 1 **132** Hospital attendants, LOC, DRWG/US - Waud (W.), no. 34 ; Hospital train interior **133** Confederate field hospital, LC-B815- 507; Naval hospital, LC-USZ62-97261; Wounded from the Battle of the Wilderness, LC-B811- 2507 **135** Stark's Louisiana Brigade fighting with Stones, National Archives **136** Battlefield of the Wilderness, LC-USZ62-65308; Difficulties of fighting in a Swamp, LC-USZ62-126180 **137** "The Rebels Retreating with their Plunder Across the Potomac River", LC-USZ62-21867; Battle of Chickamauga, LC-USZC4-4175 **138** Wounded Native Americans from Battle of the Wilderness, LC-DIG-cwpb-01550 **140** Brandy Station, VA. Headquarters, Army of the Potomac, LC-DIG-cwpb-04338 **142** Cavalry in pursuit of infantry across farm near Falling Waters, LC-DIG-ppmsca-20561 **143** Dead horses on battlefield, Gettysburg, PA, LC-USZC4-1831 **145** Fall of General Lyon, LC-USZ62-77105 **146** Massaponax Church, VA, LC-B811- 730 **148** 8th US Infantry, LOT 4190-F **149** Siege of Vicksburg, LC-DIG-pga-01871; Dead Confederate, LC-USZC4-1825 **151** Isaac and Rosa, slave children from New Orleans, LC-DIG-ppmsca-11229 **152** Returning home from Andersonville, LC-USZ62-16861; C. A. Hann parting from his family before his execution. LC-USZ62-47633 **153** Substitutes for sale, LC-USZ62-90698 **154** Notices and cartoons depicting the secession, LOC, Lot 13958; Former Vice president Breckinridge, LOC, Lot 13958 **155** Enlisting Irish and German immigrants at the Battery in New York City, LOC **156** Officers and ladies on porch of a garrison house, LC-DIG-cwpb-07514 **157** Captured flags, LC-DIG-ppmsca-21241; John H. Morgan & wife, C.S.A, LC-DIG-cwpb-03816 **158** Mrs. General M. Vickers, LC-USZ61-1842; Cartoon, LOC, LOT 4421 **159** U.S. Christian Commission. LC-DIG-cwpb-04357 **160** Francis Preston Blair and his wife, LC-USZ6-1725; Fashions for May, LC-USZ62-125366; Departure for the War, LC-USZ62-16861 **161** Family of slaves at the Gaines' house, LC-USZC4-4575; The burning of an orphan asylum during the draft riots of 1863, LC-USZ62-28701; Returning home, LC-DIG-pga-01172 **162** A mother holding hand of her son, a Union soldier, LC-USZ62-110922; Union prisoners in a Rebel town; Union recruits, LC-USZ62-36240; Woman wearing mourning brooch and displaying framed image of soldier **163** The soldier going off to war, LOC **164** Cartoon, LC-USZ62-103747; The soldier's dream of home, LC-USZC2-3014 **165** Soldier with child, LC-DIG-ppmsca-26960; Dance card from the 1861 Inaugural Ball, LC-USZ62-44644; Southern women, Illus. in AP2.L52 1863; Union refugees, LC-USZ62-42028 **166** Dance card from the 1861 Inaugural Ball, LC-USZ62-44644; Mrs. Robert E. Lee, LC-USZ62-100483; Cartoon **167** John L. Burns, the "old hero of Gettysburg," LC-B811- 2402 **168** Off for the War, LC-USZC2-2892; Fannie Virginia Casseopia Lawrence, LC-DIG-ppmsca-11481; Confederate Primer, Illus. in PE 1119.A1563 **169** Wanted, a Substitute, LOT 10615-14; The Secession Ball, LOC, Illus. in AP101.Y35 **171** Prison Opening Chapter **172** Libby Prison, LC-USZ62-38429 **173** Provost Marshal, LOC, DRWG/US - Waud, no. 55 **174** Serving out rations, LC-USZ62-703; Prisoner of War **175** Confederate prisoners at Belle Plain Landing, LOC, LOT 4181; Andersonville Prison, LC-USZ62-113730 **176** General Hill, LOC; Rampart where Hill served, LOC; Union prisoner's occupation, LC-USZ62-61115; Unknown prisoners, LC-USZ62-61115 **177** Front of "slave pen," Alexandria, VA, LC-DIG-ppmsca-11746; Alexandria, VA. Slave pen, interior view, LC-DIG-cwpb-01470; Hut, LC-DIG-cwpb-00069 **178** Andersonville prison, PGA - Morton--Bird's-eye...Andersonville; Confederate prisoners at railroad depot, LC-DIG-cwpb-02116 **179** Belle Boyd, Confederate spy, LC-BH824- 4864; Castle Thunder Prison, Petersburg, LC-DIG-ppmsca-08237 **180** Three Confederate prisoners, LC-DIG-cwpb-01451 **181** Mrs. Greenhow & Daughter, LC-DIG-cwpb-04849 **182** Wirz execution, LC-DIG-cwpb-04195 **183** Hooded body of Captain Wirz, LC-DIG-cwpb-04197 **185** Bull Run, LC-B811- 320 **186** Ruins of paper mill near Richmond, LC-USZ62-52727; Yankee Volunteers, LC-USZ62-4440 **187** Piece of flag, LC-DIG-ppmsca-30723; Grant and his Generals on horseback, LC-DIG-pga-00239 **188** Wagon train of Military Telegraph Corps, LC-DIG-cwpb-03735 **189** Confederate returns home, LOC **190** Capture of Savannah, LC-USZ62-105254; Thunderbolt Battery, LC-DIG-ppmsca-22511 **193** Cartoon, LOC, LOT 4421 **192** View of Fort McAllister, LC-DIG-cwpb-03485 **193** Southern "Volunteer", LOC, LOT 4421; Bombardment of Fort Fisher, LC-USZC2-1986 **194** The Dictator, LC-DIG-cwpb-01238 **196** Antietam, LOC; Cedar Mountain, LOC **197** Railroad Gun, LC-DIG-cwpb-01368 **198** Confederate soldiers as they fell inside the fence on the Hagerstown road, LC-DIG-cwpb-01092 **200** Portraits from Liljenquist Collection, LOC, DLC/ PP-2010:105 **201** Letter from Sherman, National Archives; General Sherman's Advance, Georgia, LC-USZ62-83284; General Sherman's Advance, Kenesaw, LC-USZ62-83282 **203** Soldier's Cemetery, LC-DIG-cwpb-03928 **204** Charleston, SC, LC-B811- 3104; Richmond, VA, LC-B811- 3254 **205** Front page of New York Times, LC-USZ62-50040; Jefferson Davis! "As women and children.", LC-DIG-ppmsca-23862 **206** Lewis Payne, LC-B817- 7775; Lewis Payne, LC-B817- 7777 **207** Spectators at side of the Capitol, LC-B817- 7748; Deathbed of Lincoln, LC-DIG-npcc-19613 **208** Graves of sailors, LC-B811- 187; Boxcars with refugees at railroad depot, LC-B811- 3671 **209** Men repairing single-track railroad, LC-B811- 2663 **211** Family arriving at Union Lines, LC-DIG-cwpb-01161; Proclamation of Emancipation, LC-USZ62-102573; The lost cause, reproduction LC-USZ62-15649 **212** General Edward O.C. Ord, wife and, LC-B811- 3384 **213** The last offer of reconciliation, LC-DIG-ppmsca-19257; Interior of Fort Sumpter, LOT 4166-D **214** Atlanta, Georgia. Sherman's men destroying railroad, LC-B811- 3631; The true story of the capture of Jeff. Davis, PC/US - 1865.G4515, no. 2b **215** The Lost Cause, LC-DIG-pga-01734 **216** Composite of scenes, LC-USZ62-98263 **217** "Radical" members, LC-DIG-ppmsca-30572 **218** Surrender of Robert E. Lee, LC-USZ62-127691 **219** Home from the war, LOT 4420

Cover photos
Folder cover: Upper photo, Library of Congress, AMB/TIN no. 2279; Lower photo courtesy of The Museum of the Confederacy; Back cover: Library of Congress, LC-B813-1613 B; The Museum of the Confederacy;

Book Cover & Pocket: The last charge at the Battle of Shiloh,LC-USDZ62-48871

DVD Cover: Front page of New York Times, LC-USZ62-50040; Library of Congress, AMB/TIN no.2315

INDEX